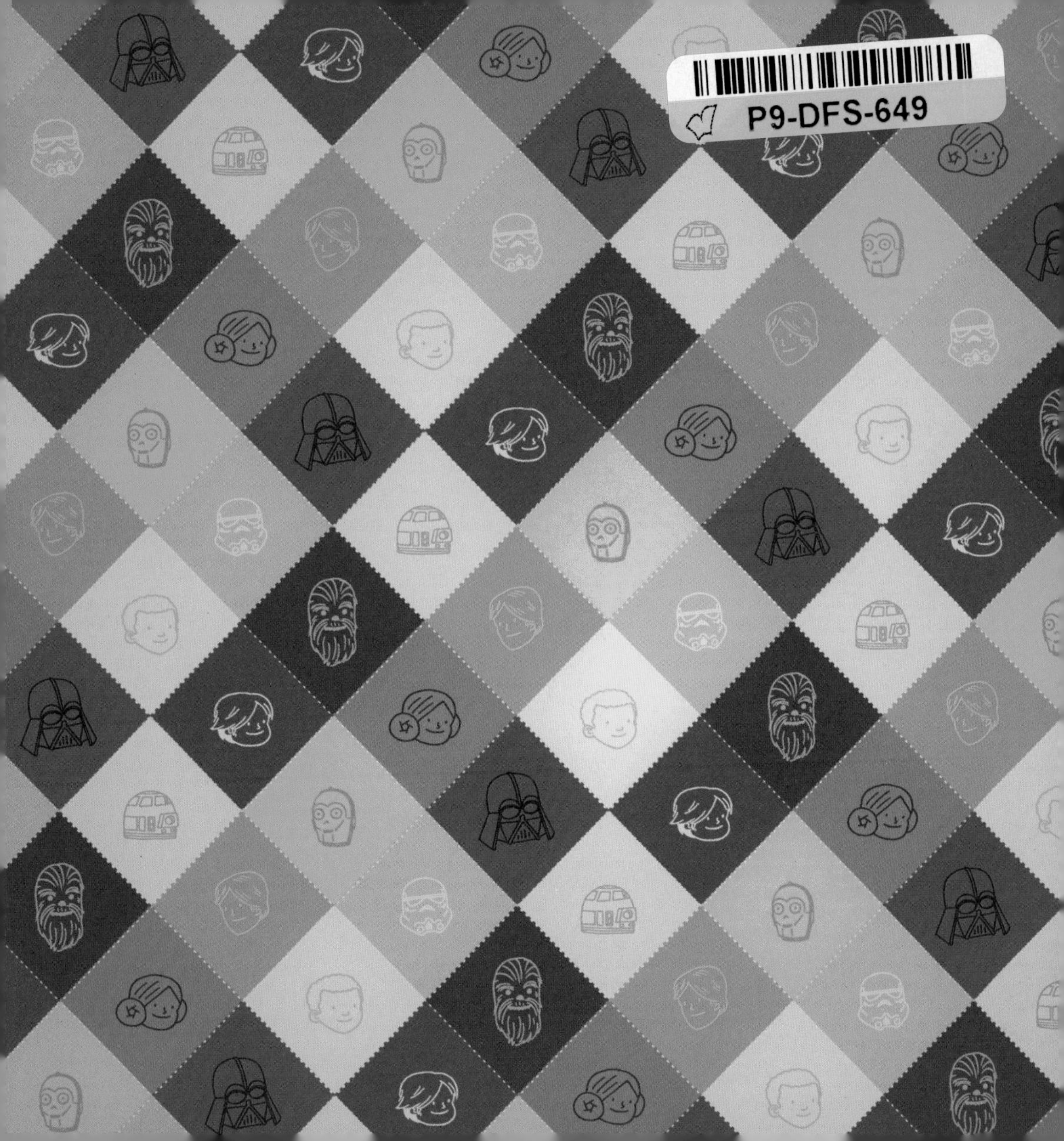

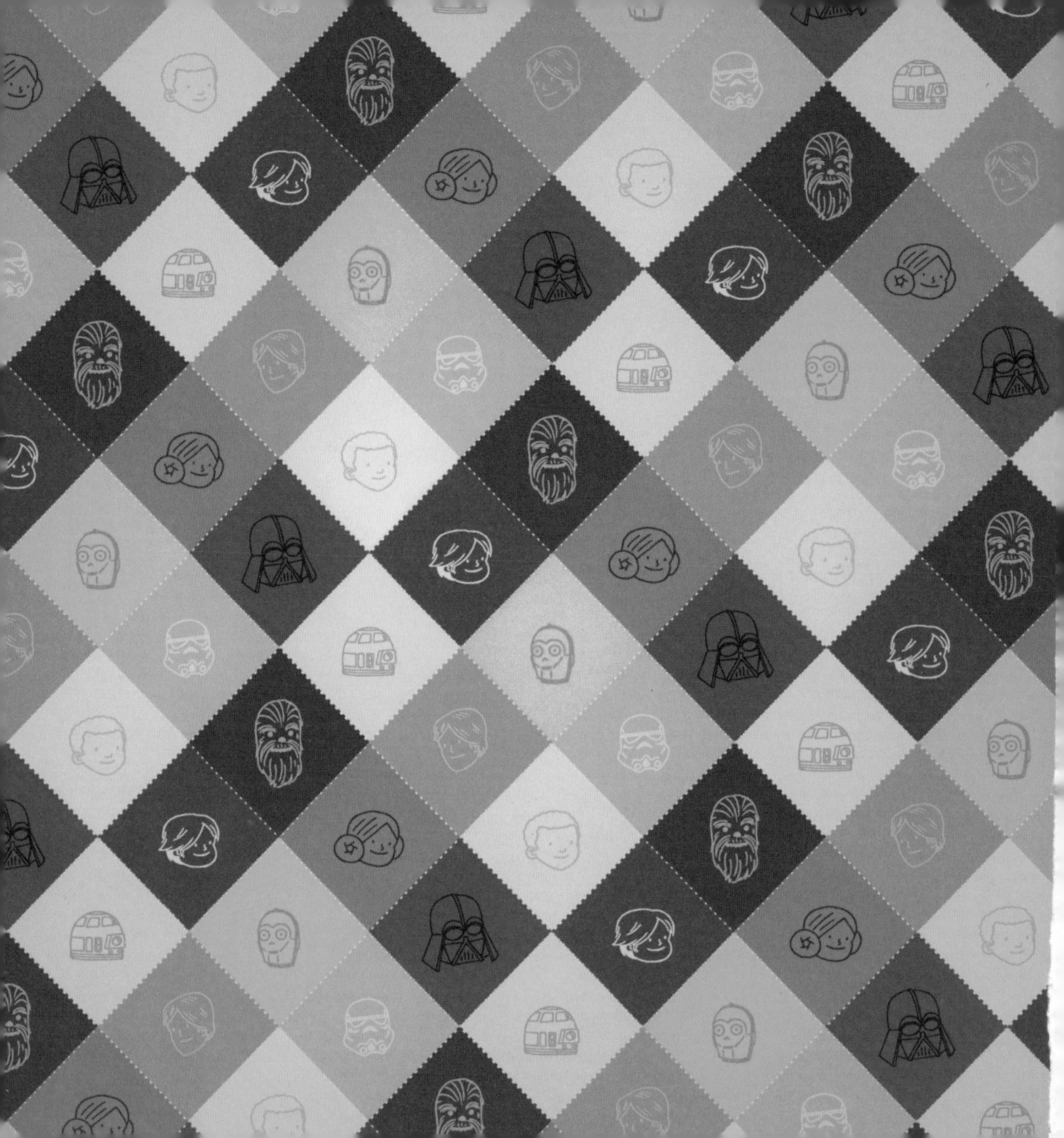

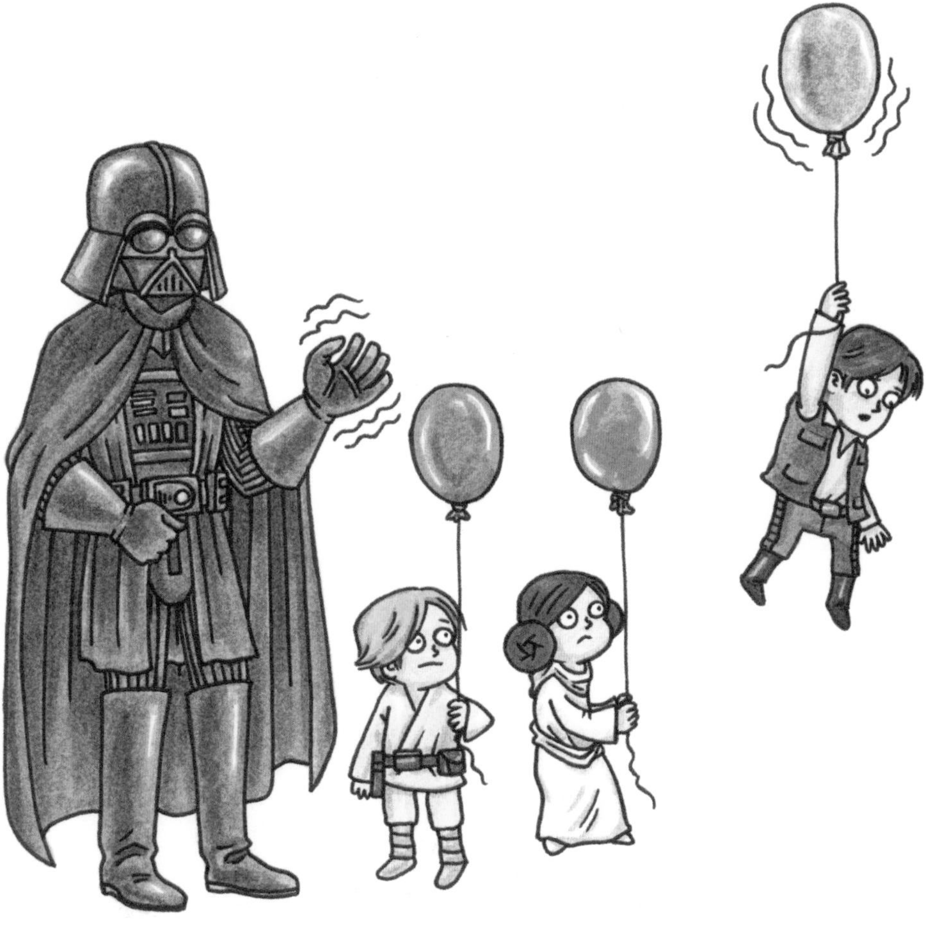

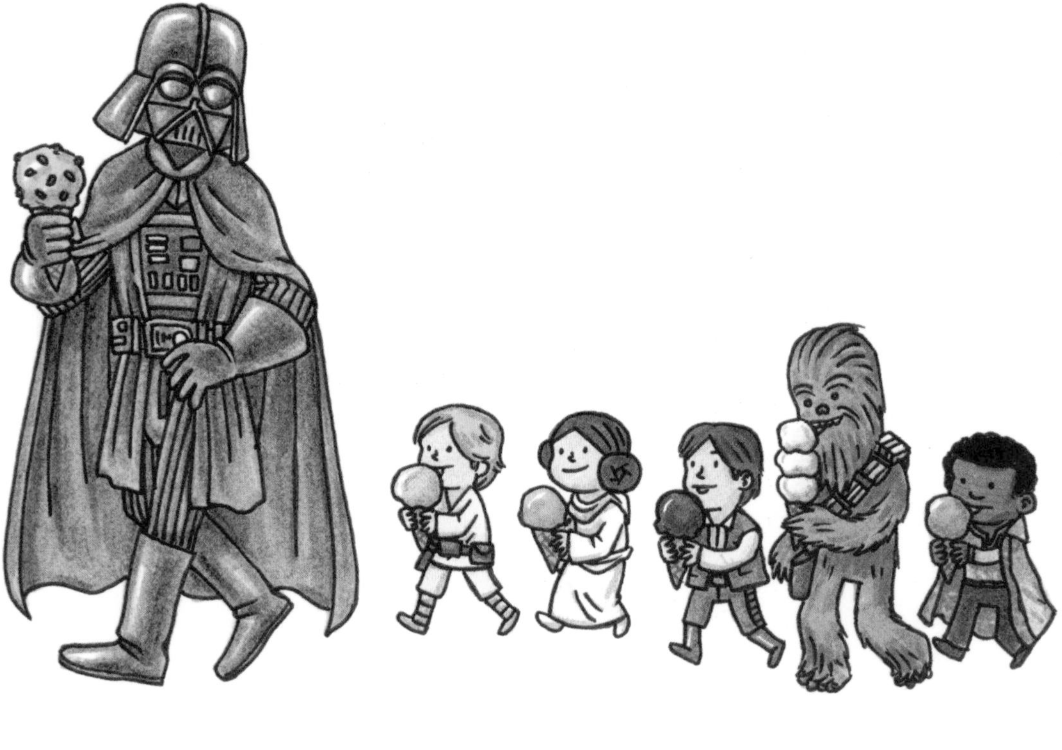

DARTH VADER™

and Friends

JEFFREY BROWN

CHRONICLE BOOKS
SAN FRANCISCO

LIBRARY OF CONGRESS CATALOGING-IN-PUBLICATION DATA IS AVAILABLE.

ISBN: 978-1-4521-3810-7

MANUFACTURED IN CHINA.
WRITTEN AND DRAWN BY JEFFREY BROWN.
DESIGNED BY MICHAEL MORRIS.

THANKS TO STEVE MOCKUS, J.W. RINZLER, MARC GERALD, MY FAMILY, AND ALL OF MY READERS. SPECIAL THANKS TO RYAN GERMICK AND MICHEAL LOPEZ AT GOOGLE FOR THE ORIGINAL INSPIRATION TO MAKE DARTH VADER AND SON.

10 9 8 7 6 5 4

CHRONICLE BOOKS LLC
680 SECOND STREET
SAN FRANCISCO, CALIFORNIA 94107

WWW.CHRONICLEBOOKS.COM

WWW.STARWARS.COM

MIX
Paper from
responsible sources
FSC™ C020056

A long time ago in a galaxy far, far away....

Episode BFF:
DARTH VADER AND FRIENDS
While ruling the Galactic Empire, Lord Darth Vader aims to crush the Rebel Alliance with a little help from his friends. His twin children, Luke and Leia, have other plans- and powerful friends of their own....

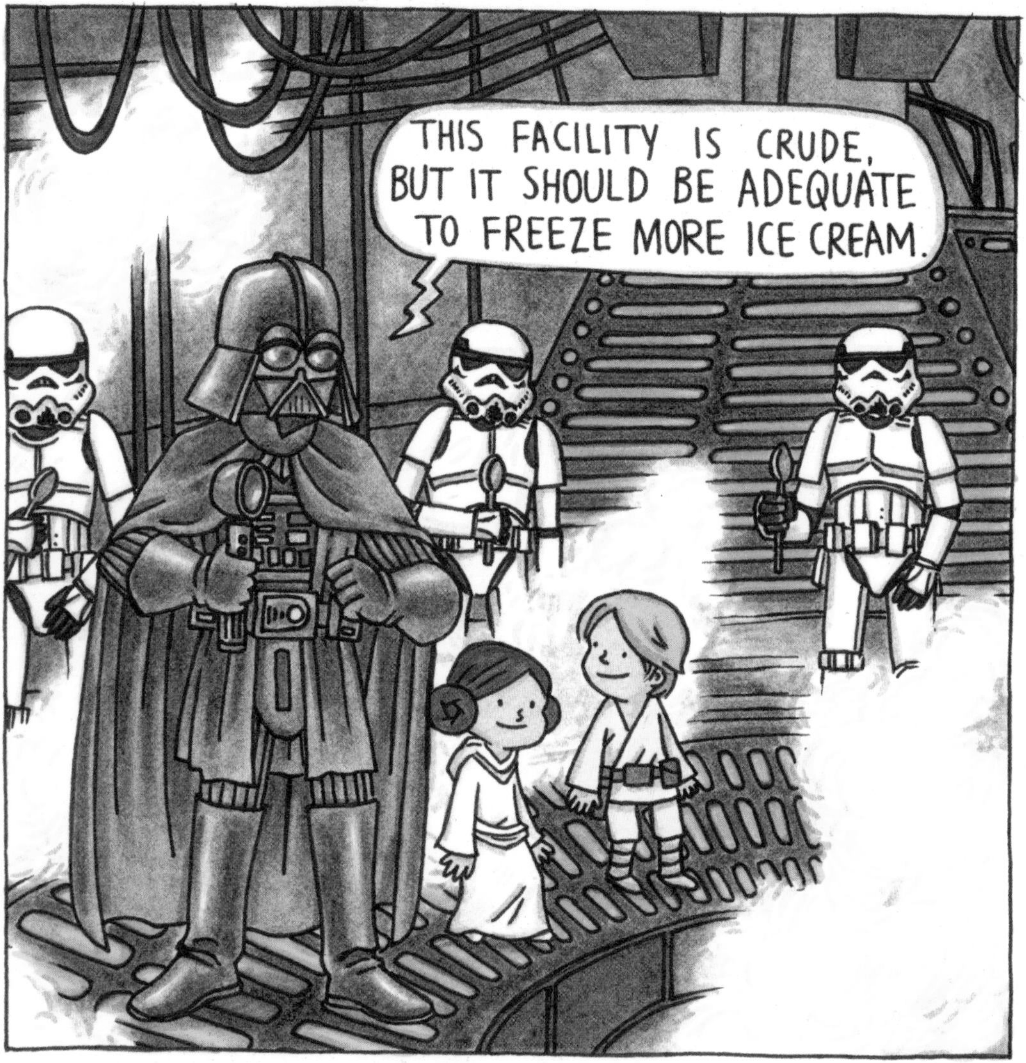
THIS FACILITY IS CRUDE, BUT IT SHOULD BE ADEQUATE TO FREEZE MORE ICE CREAM.

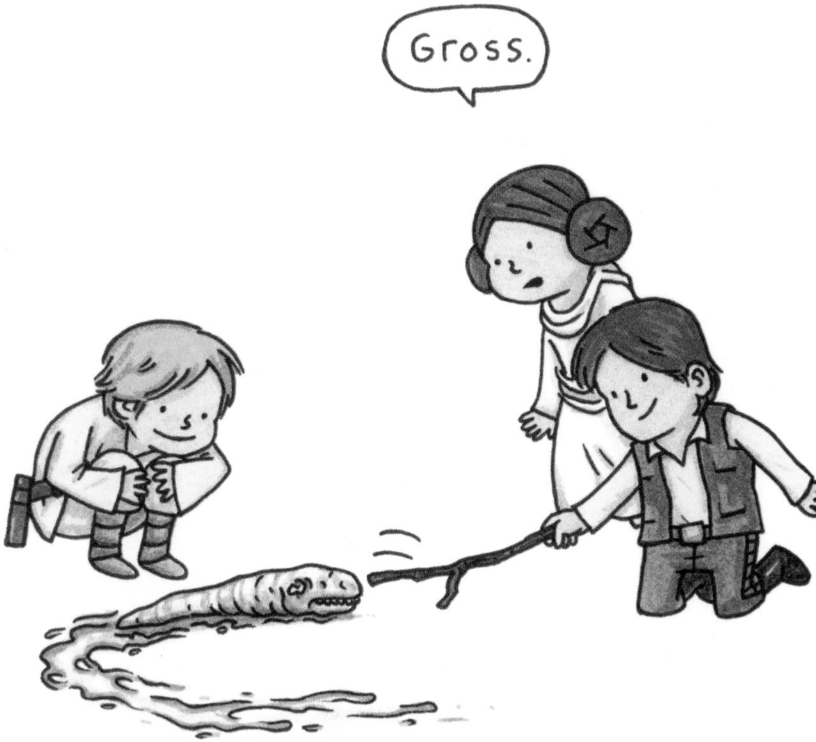
Gross.

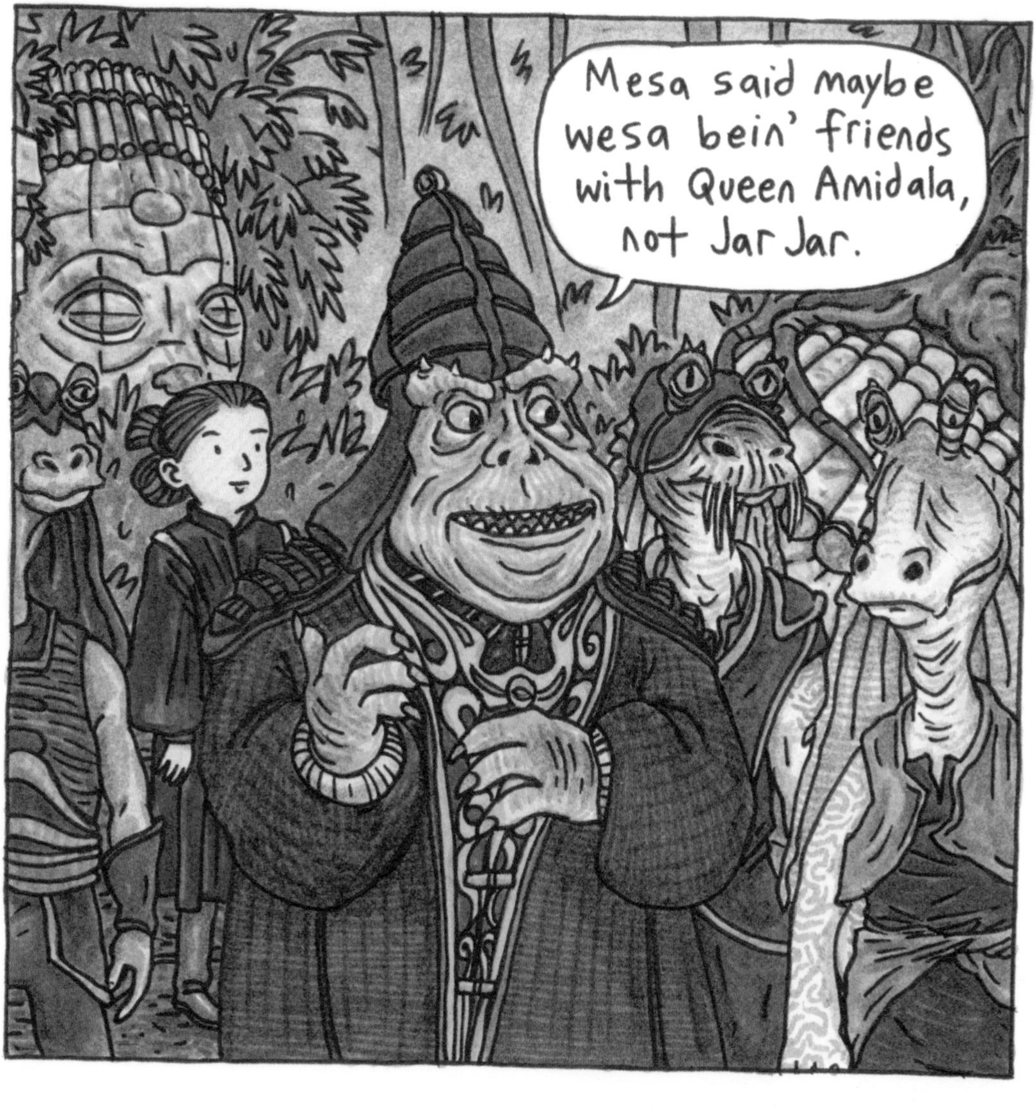
Mesa said maybe wesa bein' friends with Queen Amidala, not Jar Jar.

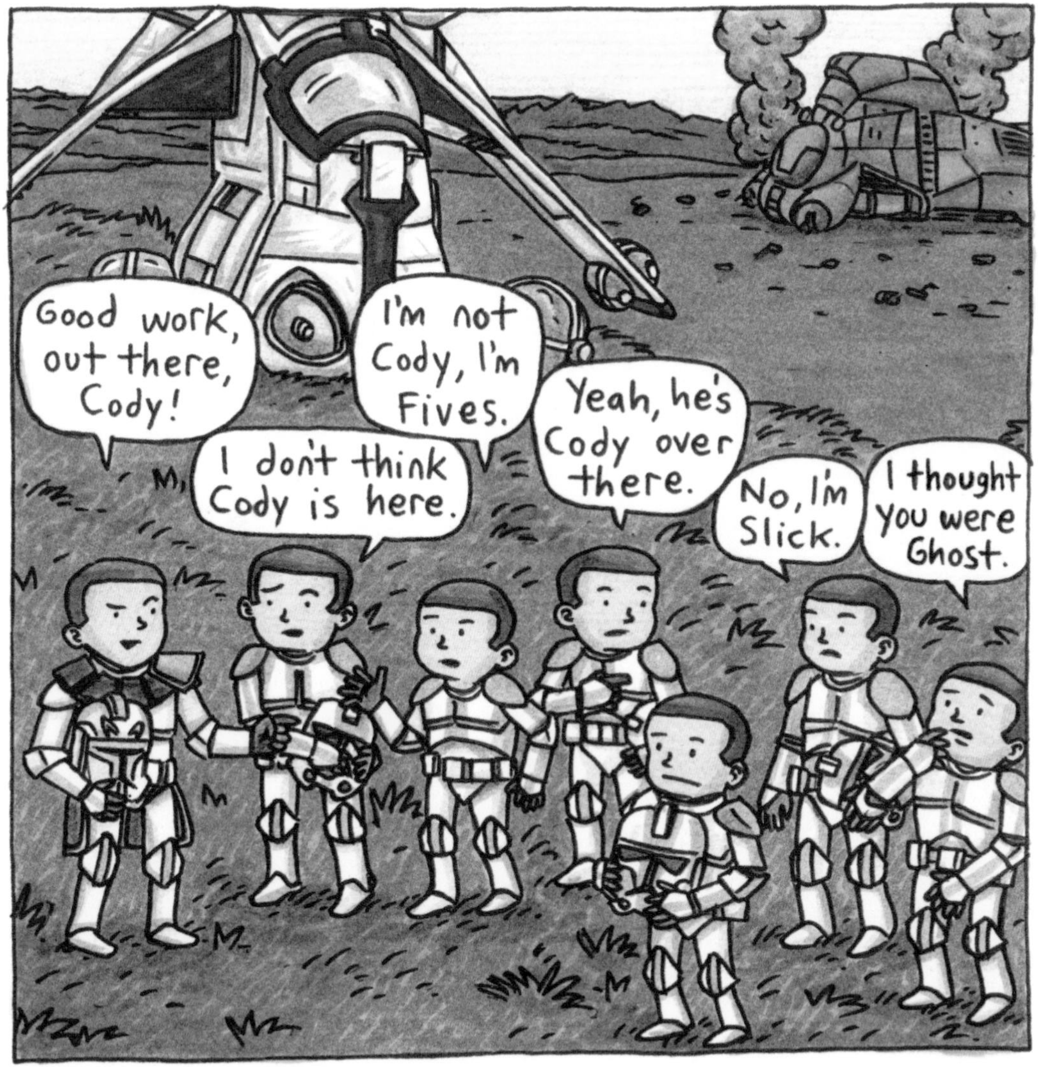
Good work, out there, Cody!
I'm not Cody, I'm Fives.
I don't think Cody is here.
Yeah, he's Cody over there.
No, I'm Slick.
I thought you were Ghost.

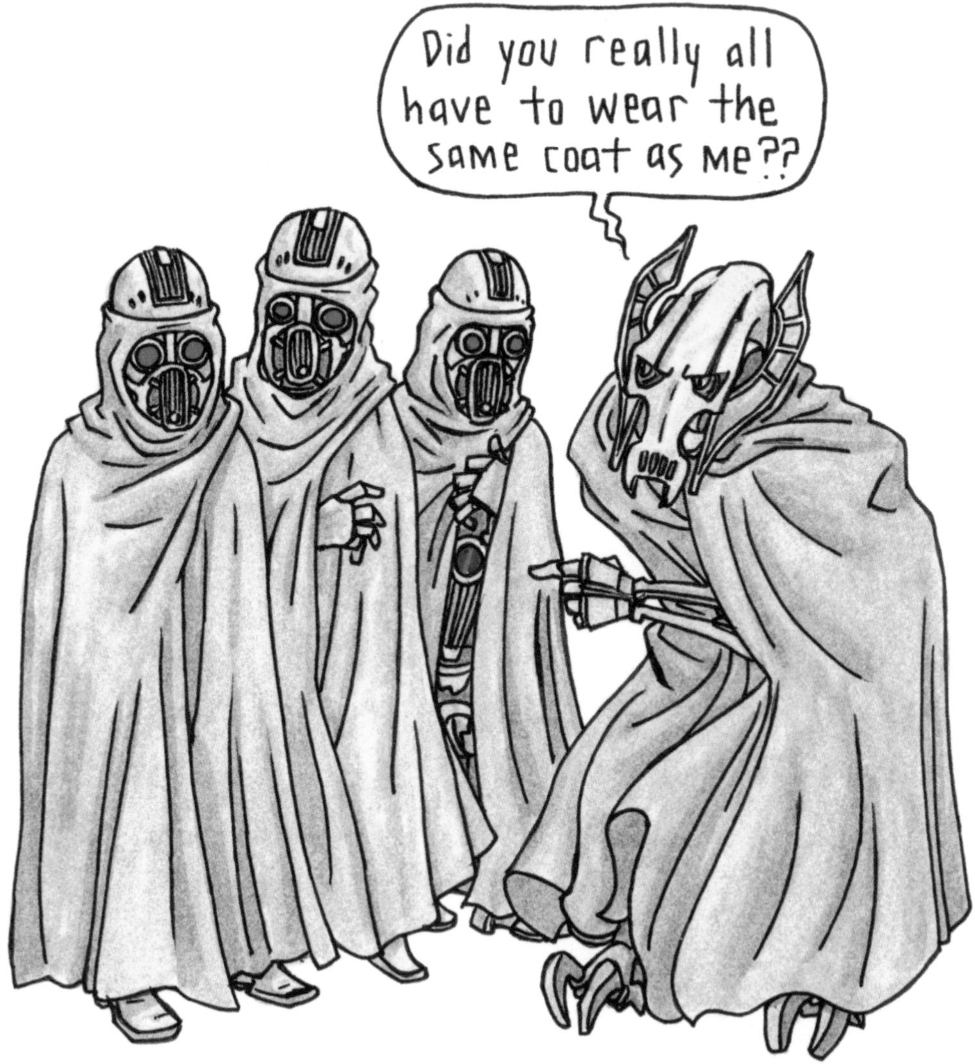
Did you really all have to wear the same coat as me??

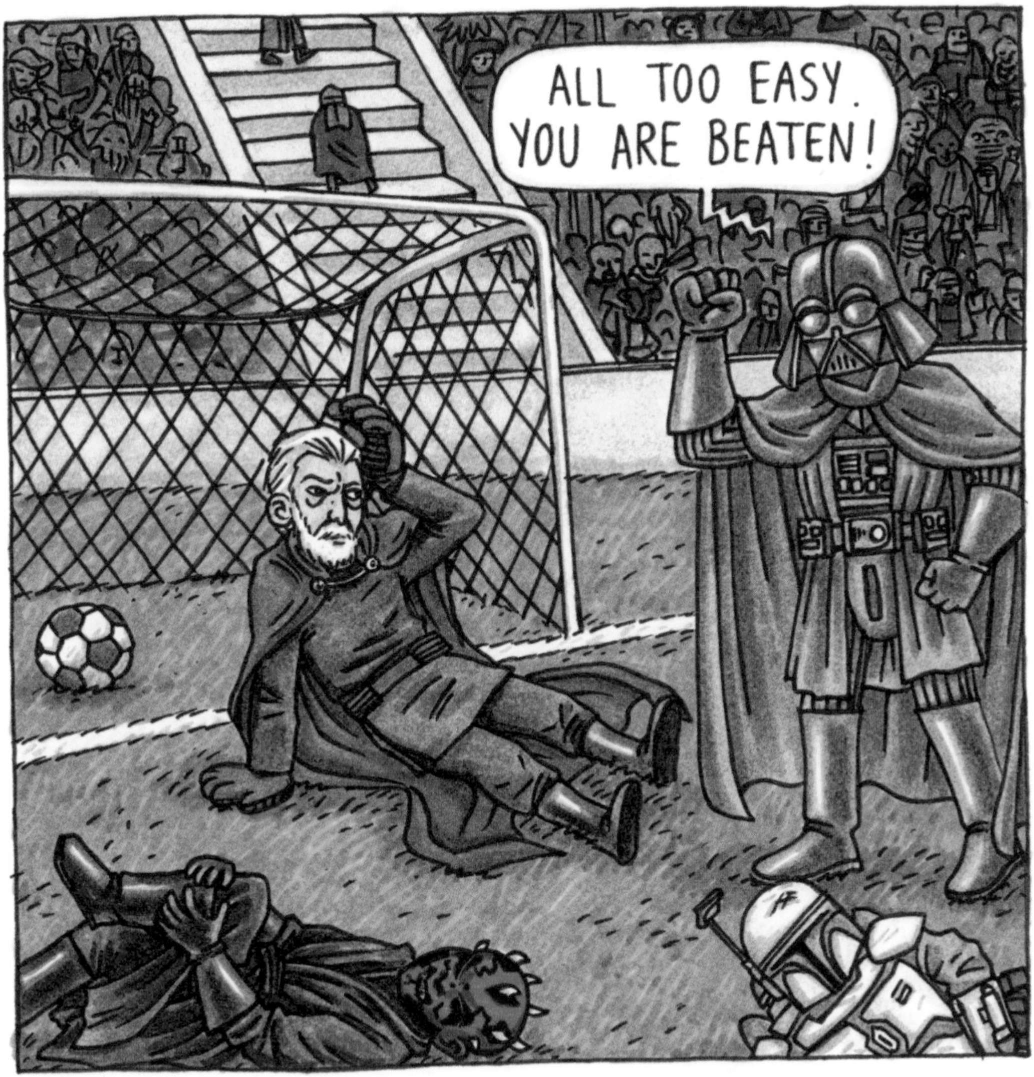
ALL TOO EASY. YOU ARE BEATEN!

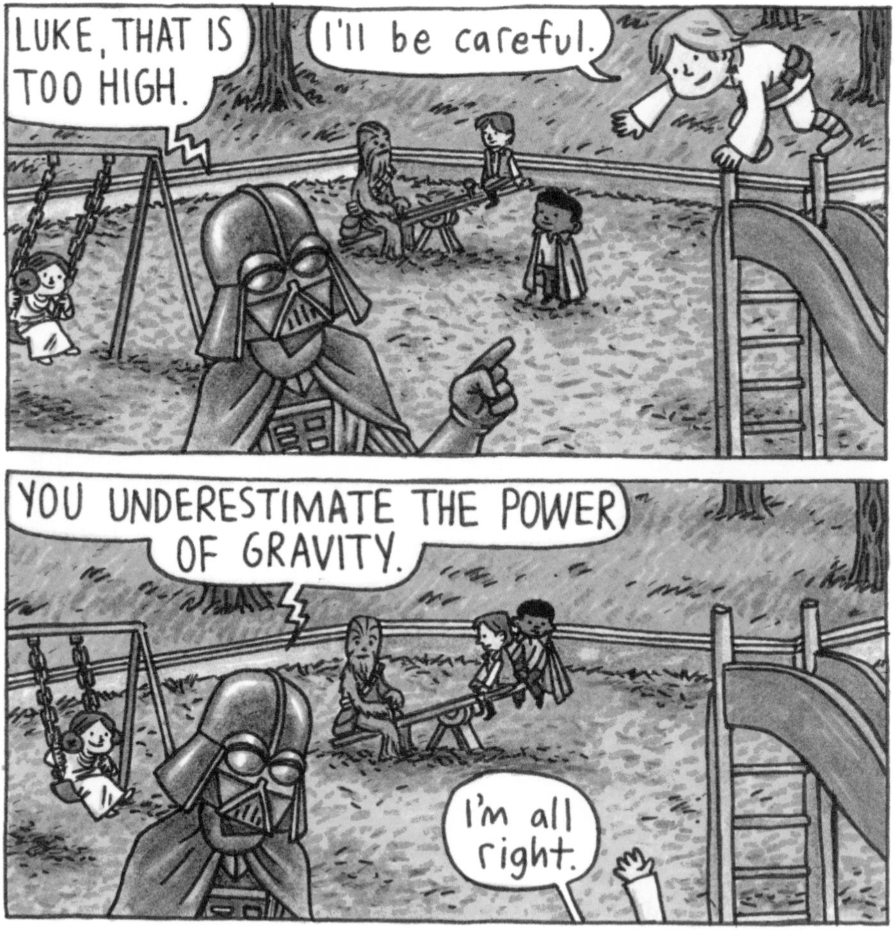
LUKE, THAT IS TOO HIGH.
I'll be careful.
YOU UNDERESTIMATE THE POWER OF GRAVITY.
I'm all right.

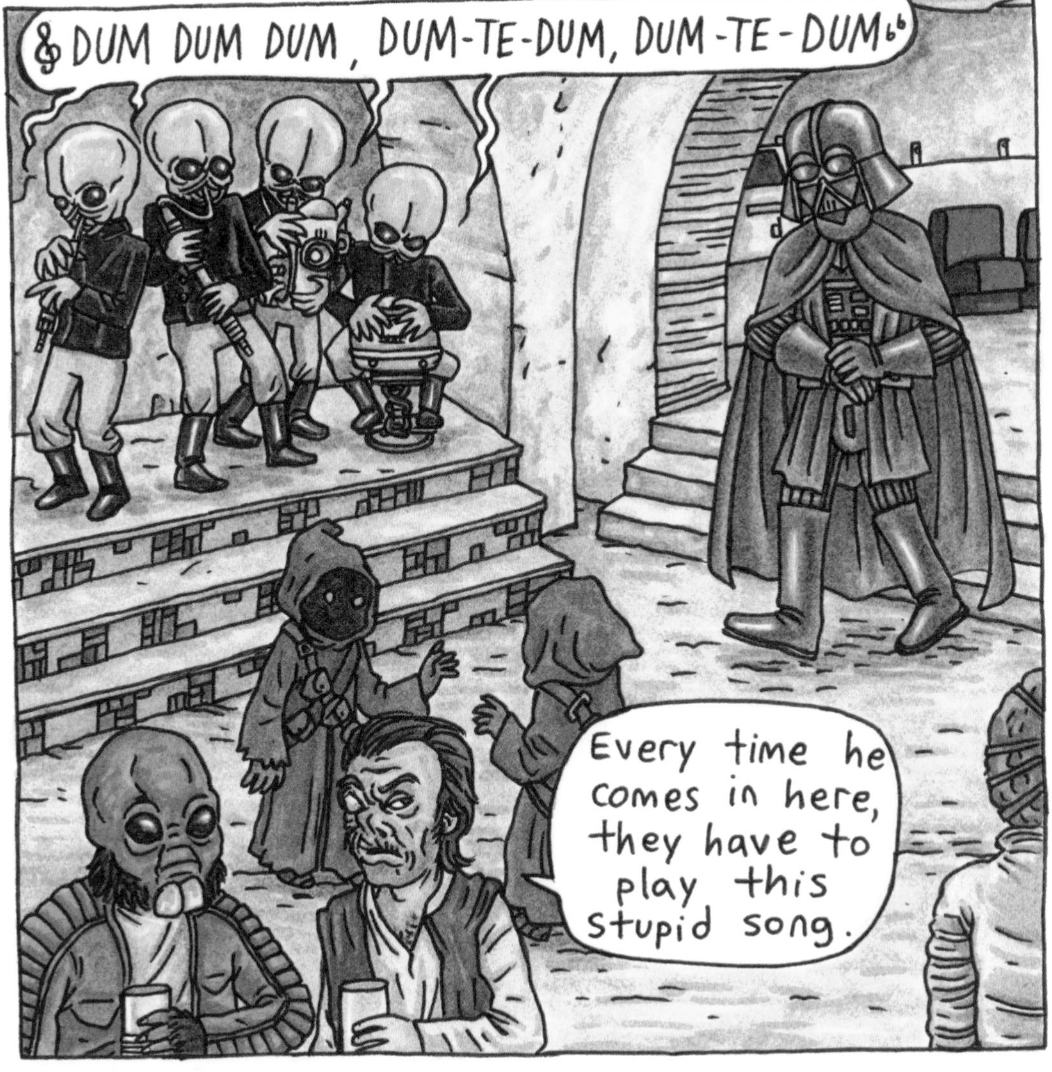
DUM DUM DUM, DUM-TE-DUM, DUM-TE-DUM
Every time he comes in here, they have to play this stupid song.

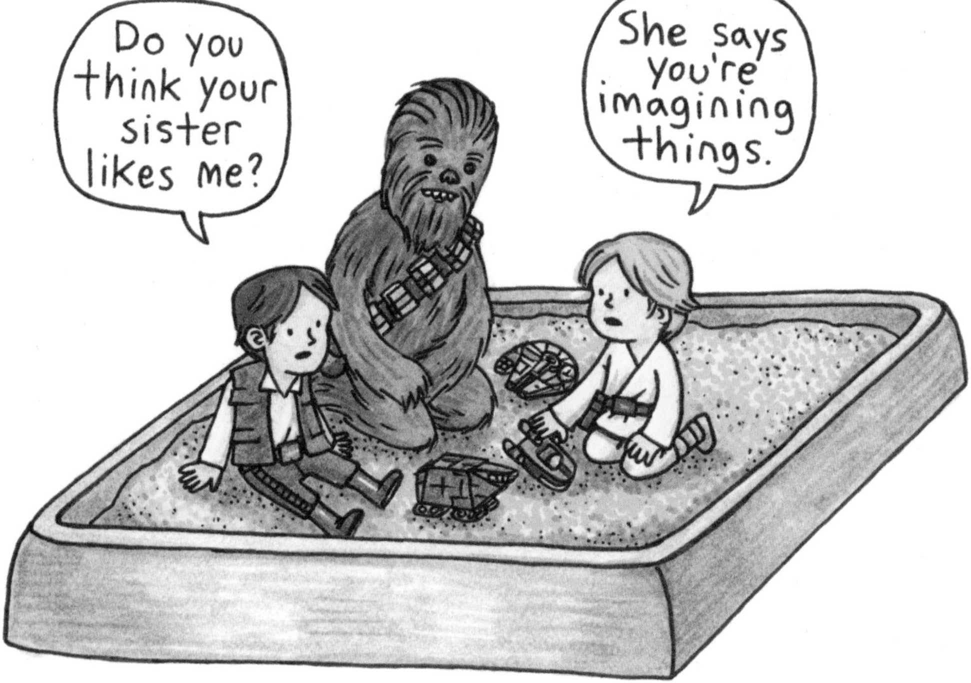
Do you think your sister likes me?
She says you're imagining things.

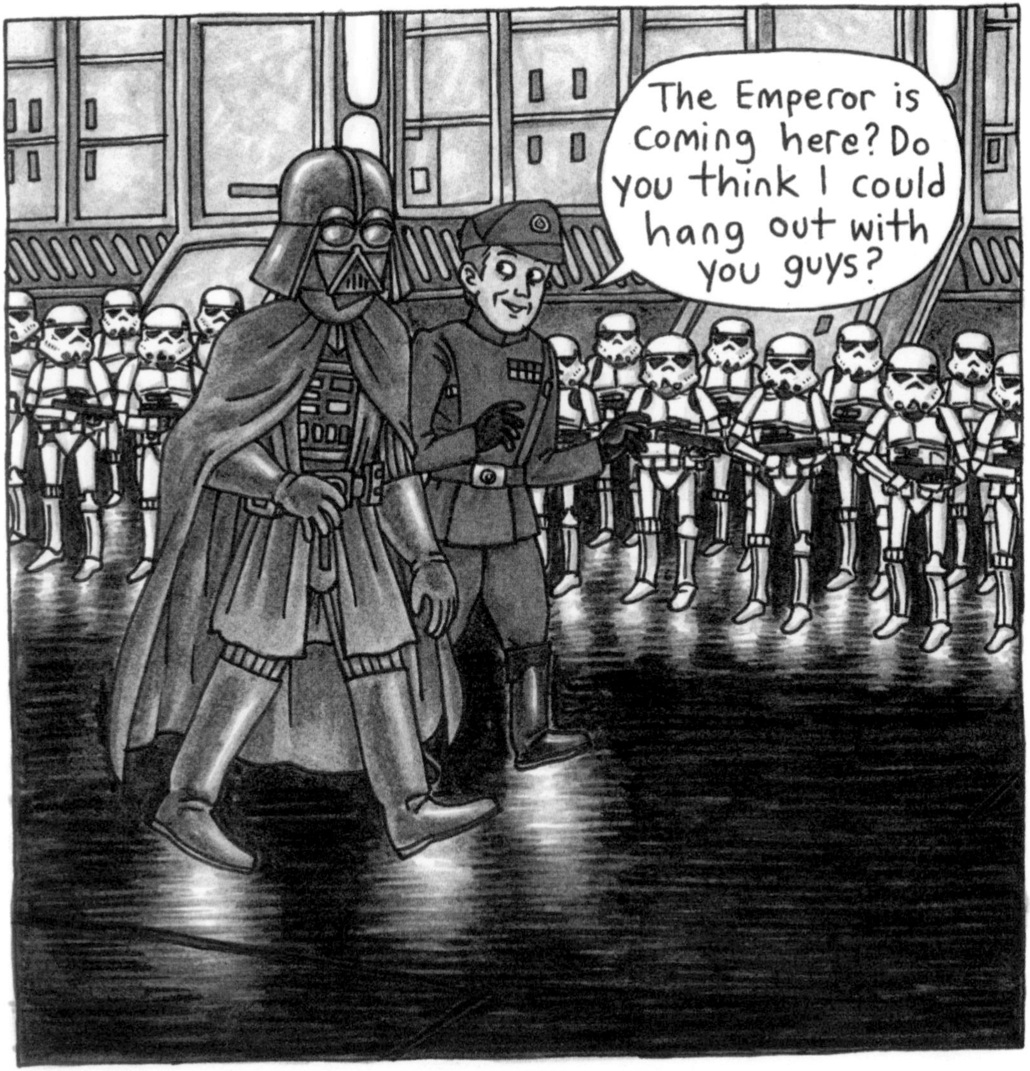
The Emperor is coming here? Do you think I could hang out with you guys?

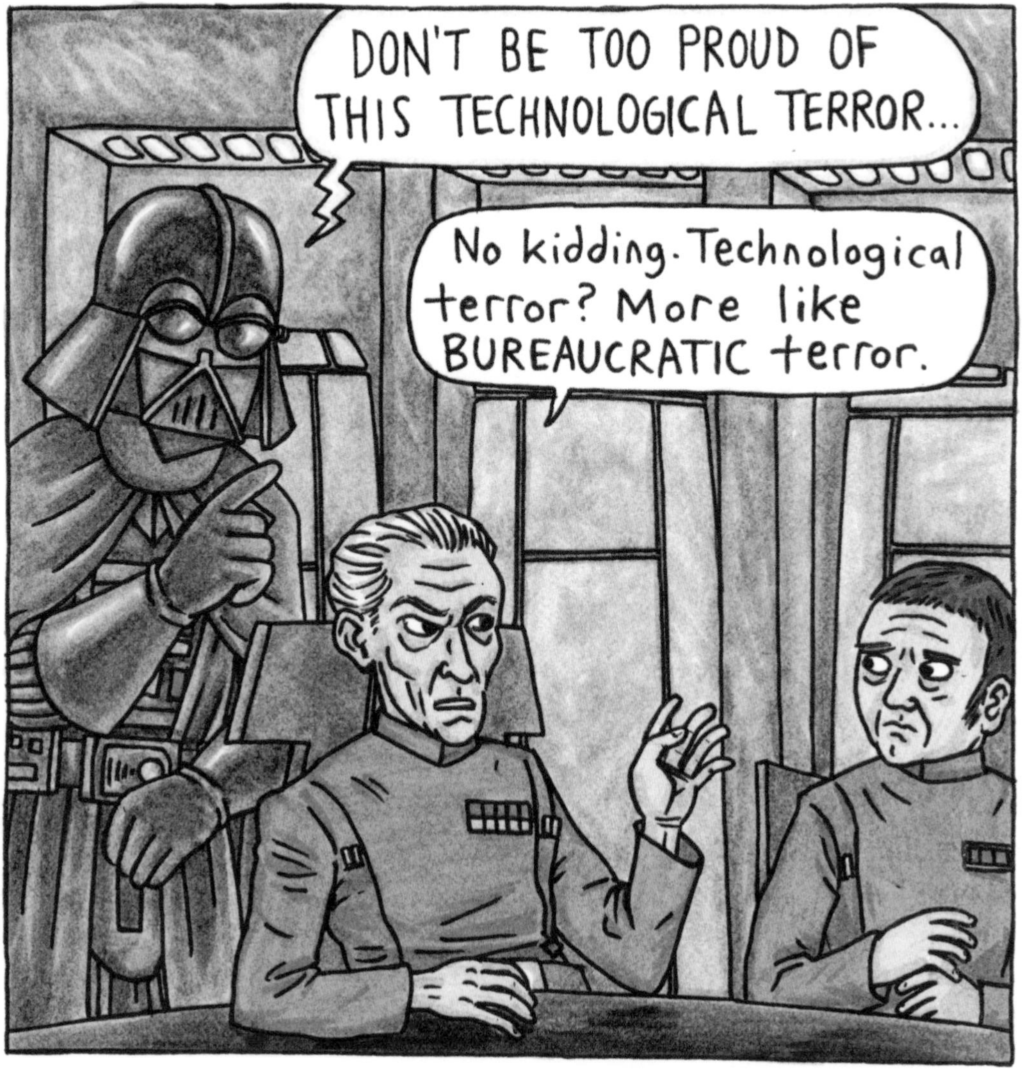
DON'T BE TOO PROUD OF THIS TECHNOLOGICAL TERROR...
No kidding. Technological terror? More like BUREAUCRATIC terror.

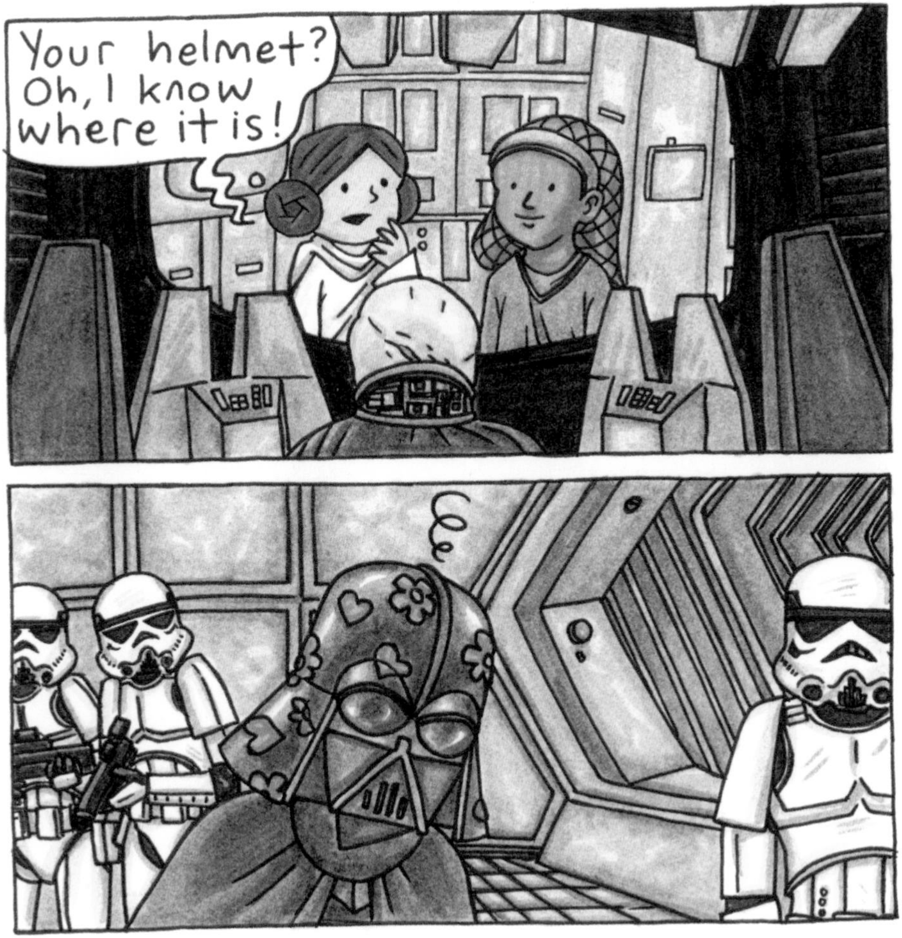
Your helmet? Oh, I know where it is!

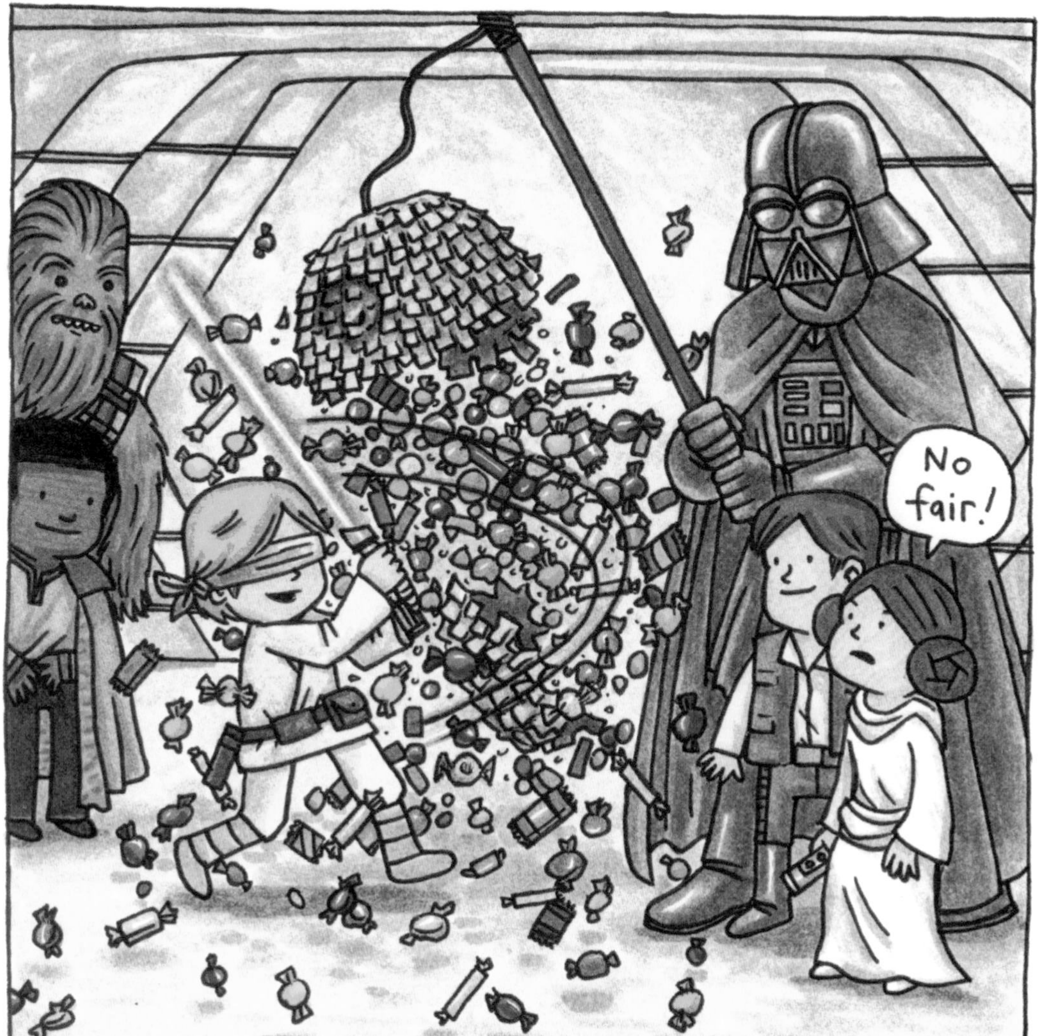
No fair!

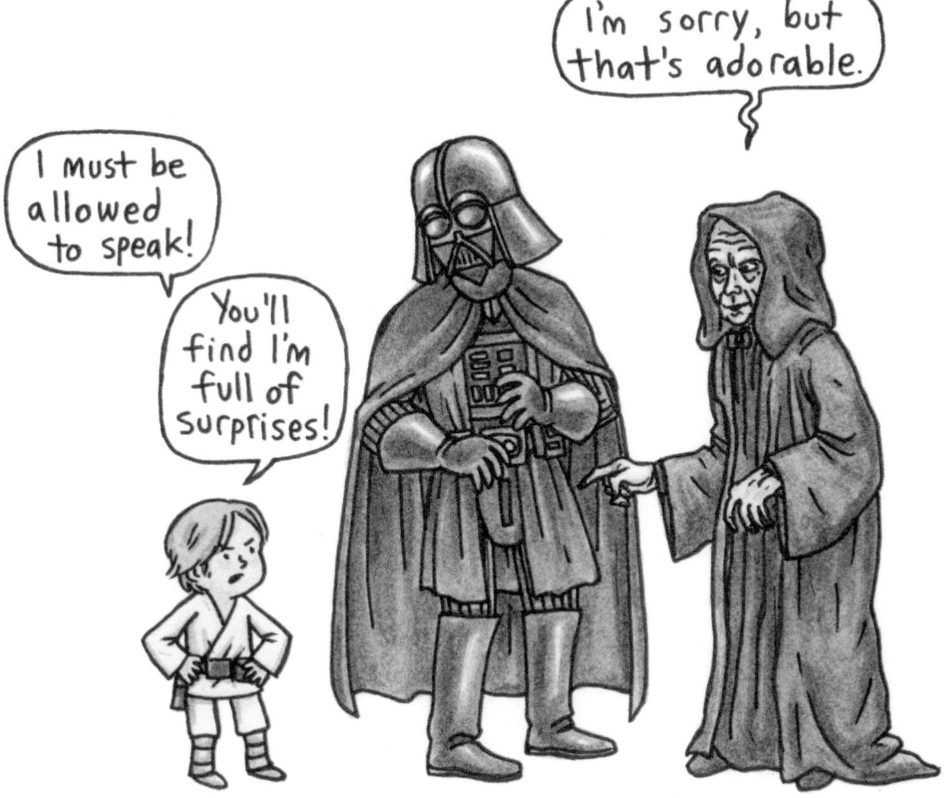
I must be allowed to speak!
You'll find I'm full of surprises!
I'm sorry, but that's adorable.

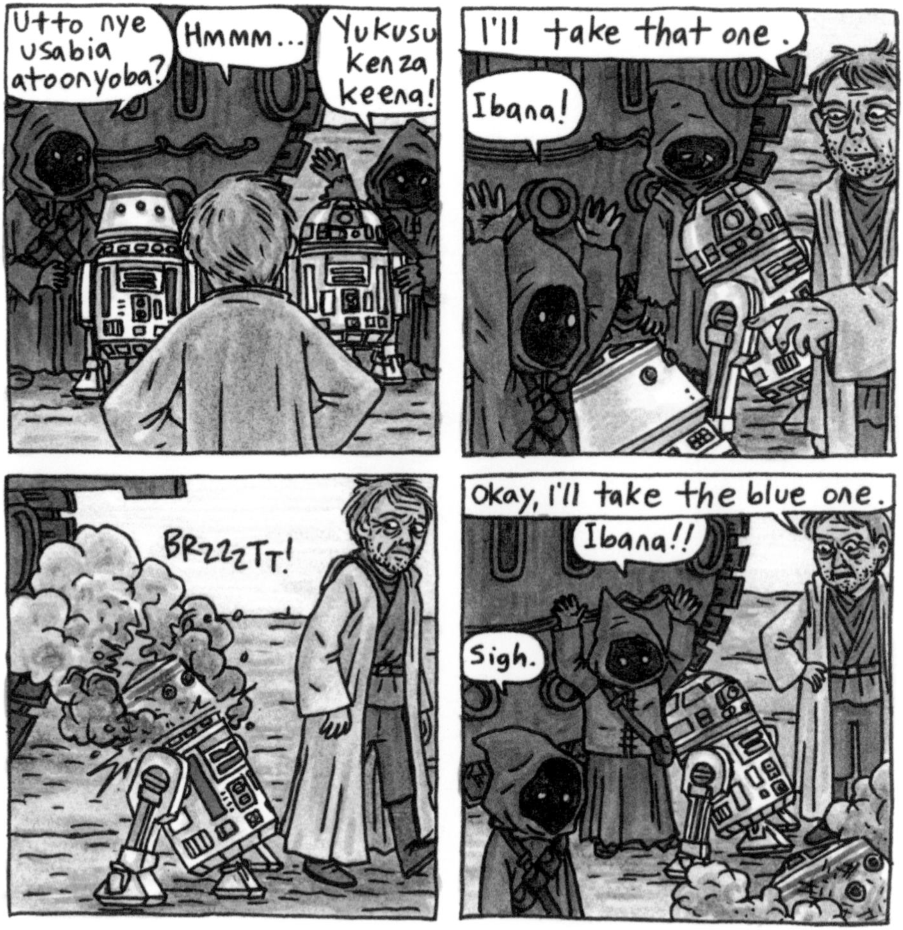
Utto nye usabia atoonyoba?
Hmmm...
Yukusu kenza keena!
I'll take that one.
Ibana!
BRZZZZTT!
Okay, I'll take the blue one.
Ibana!!
Sigh.

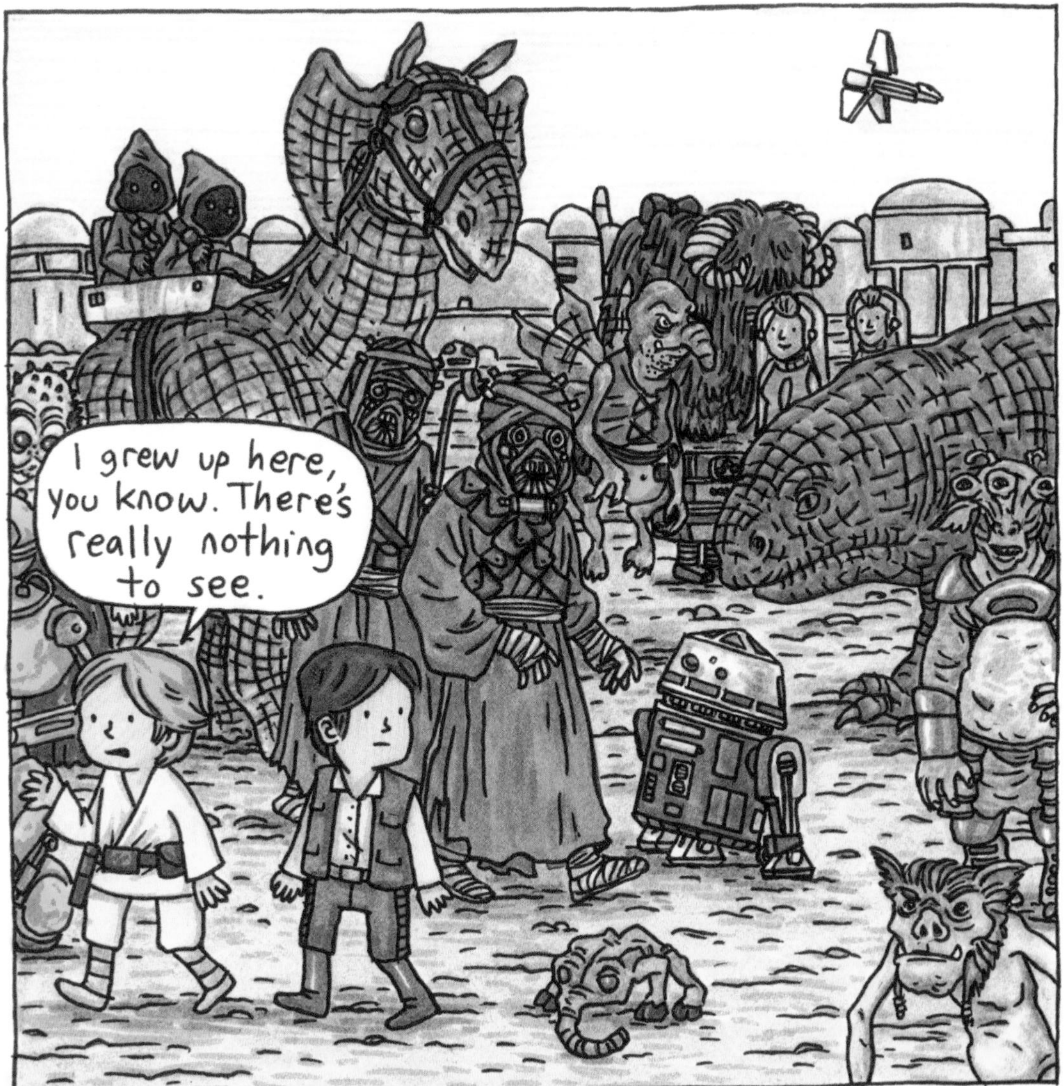
I grew up here, you know. There's really nothing to see.

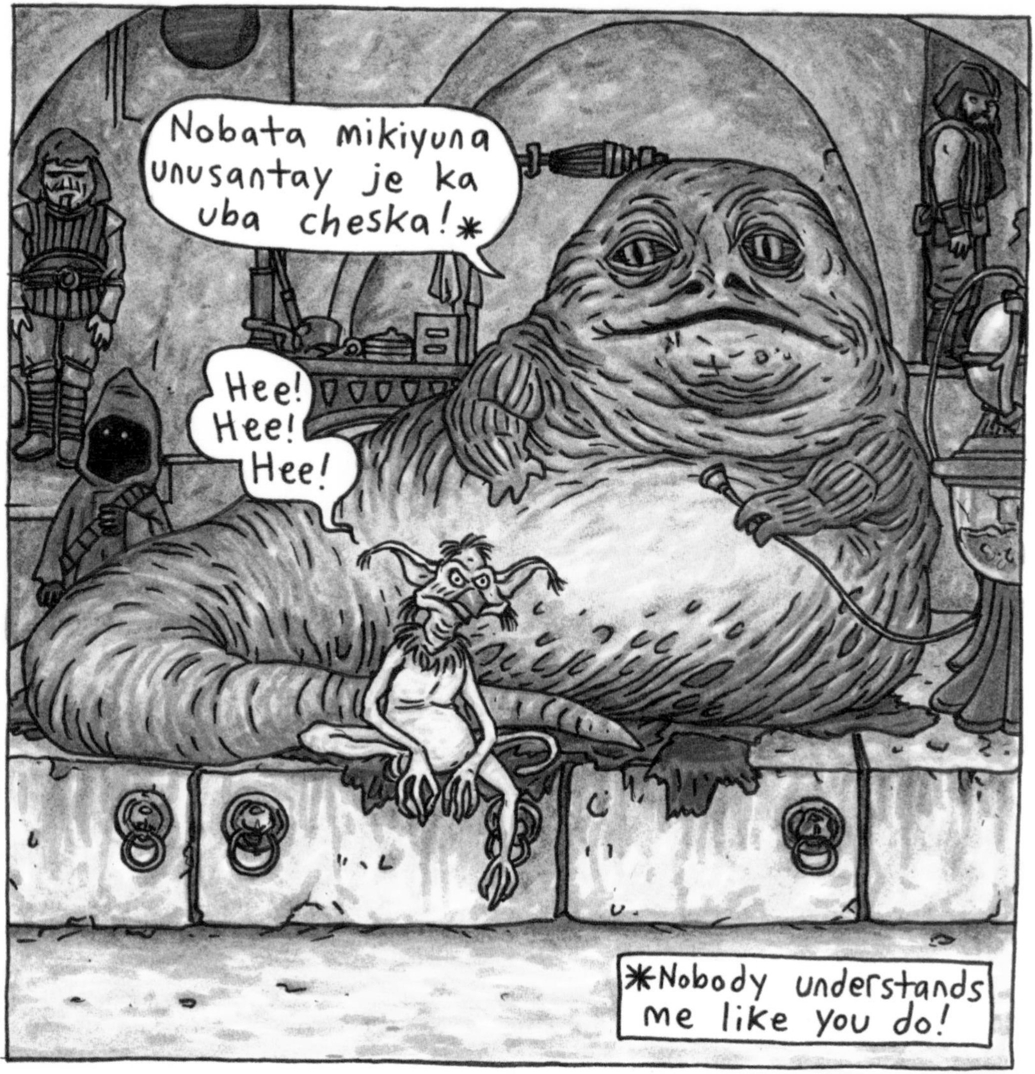
Nobata mikiyuna unusantay je ka uba cheska!*
Hee! Hee! Hee!
*Nobody understands me like you do!

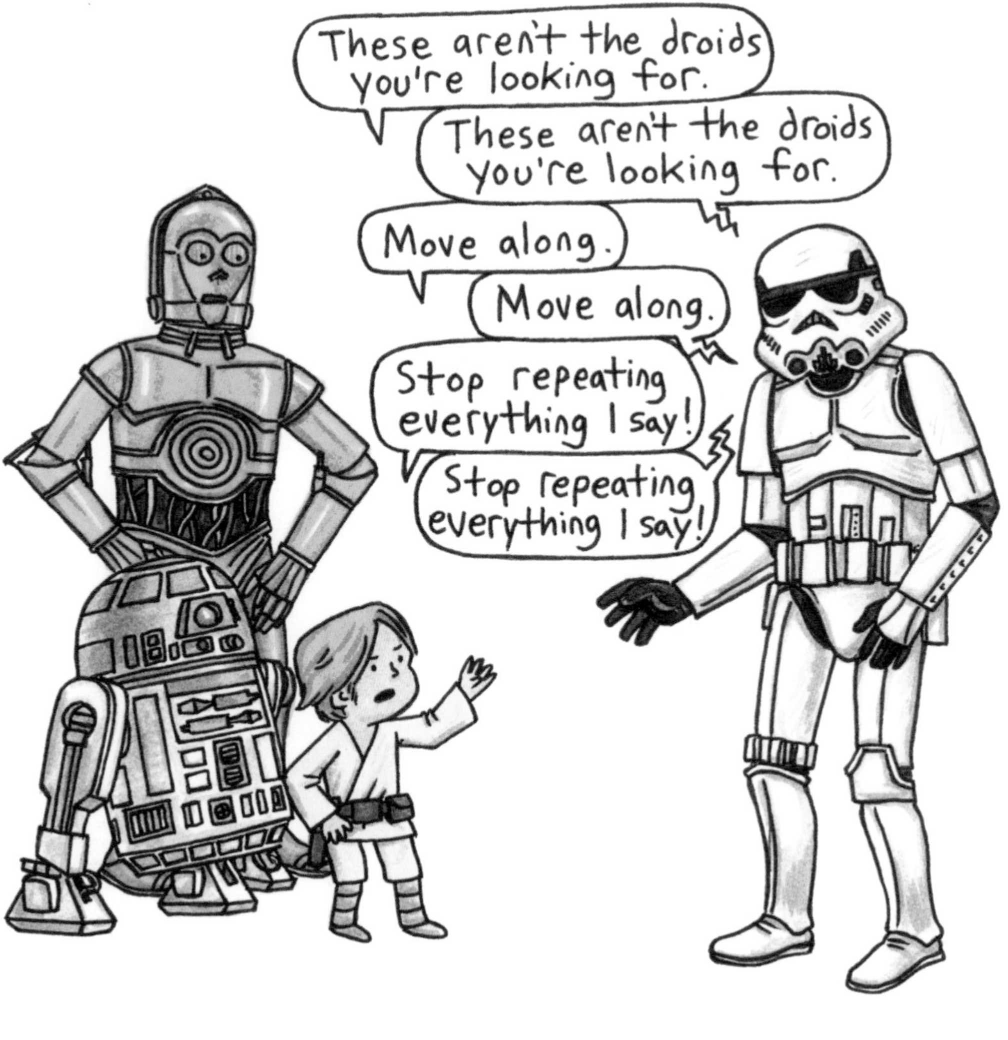
These aren't the droids you're looking for.
These aren't the droids you're looking for.
Move along.
Move along.
Stop repeating everything I say!
Stop repeating everything I say!

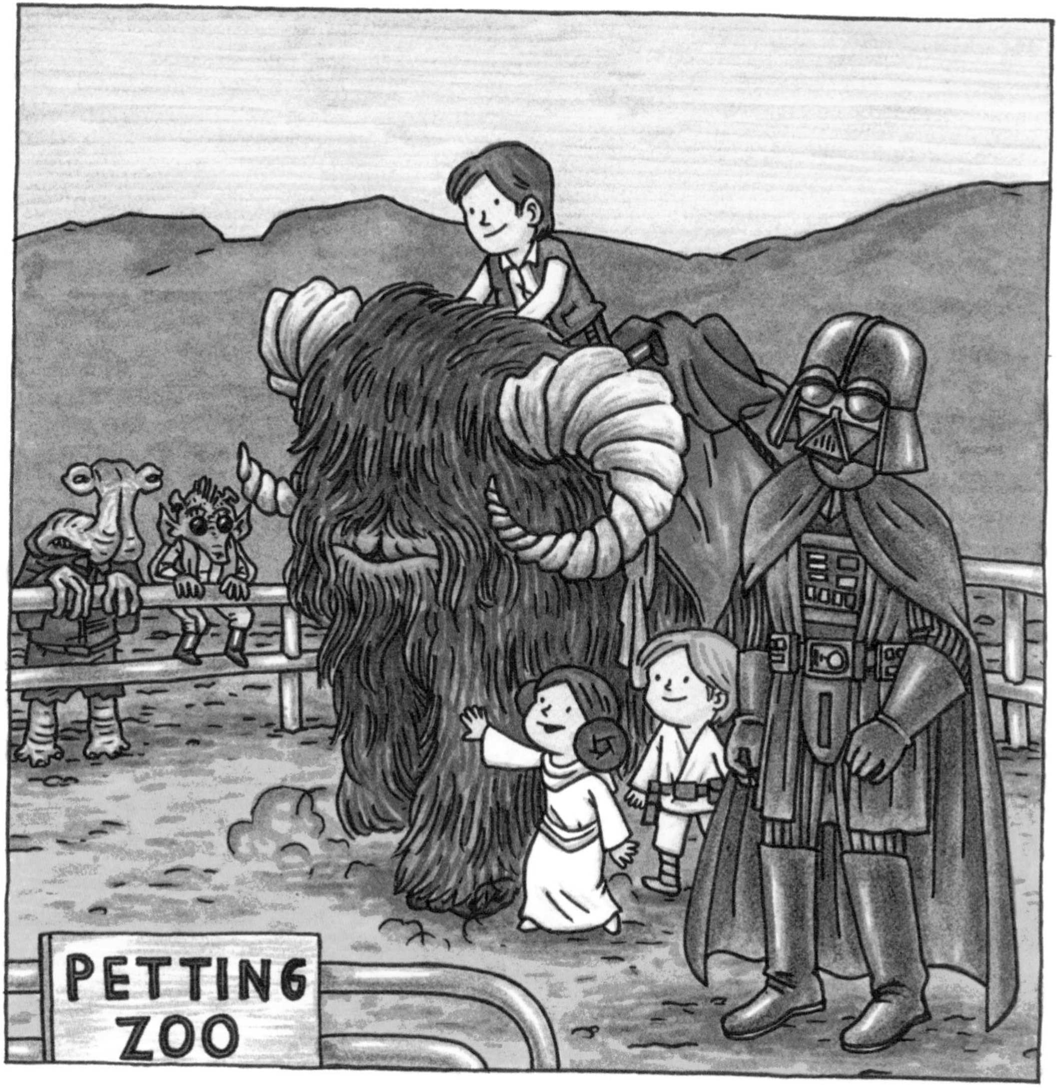
PETTING
ZOO

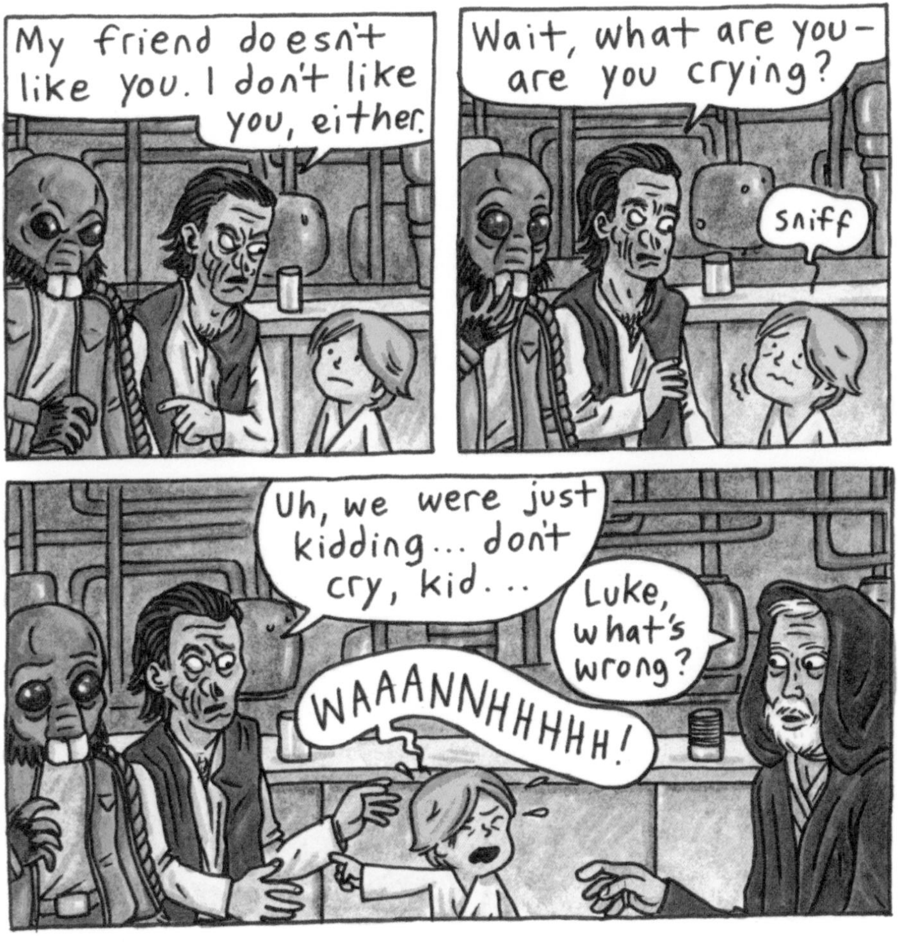
My friend doesn't like you. I don't like you, either.
Wait, what are you- are you crying?
sniff
Uh, we were just kidding... don't cry, kid...
Luke, what's wrong?
WAAANNHHHHHH!

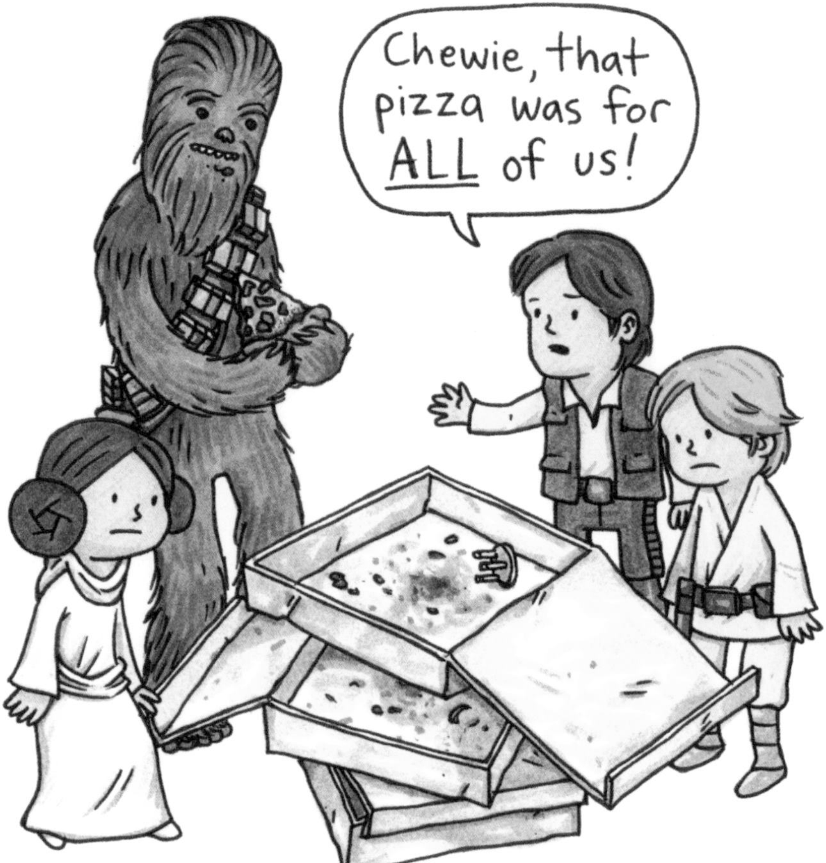
Chewie, that pizza was for ALL of us!

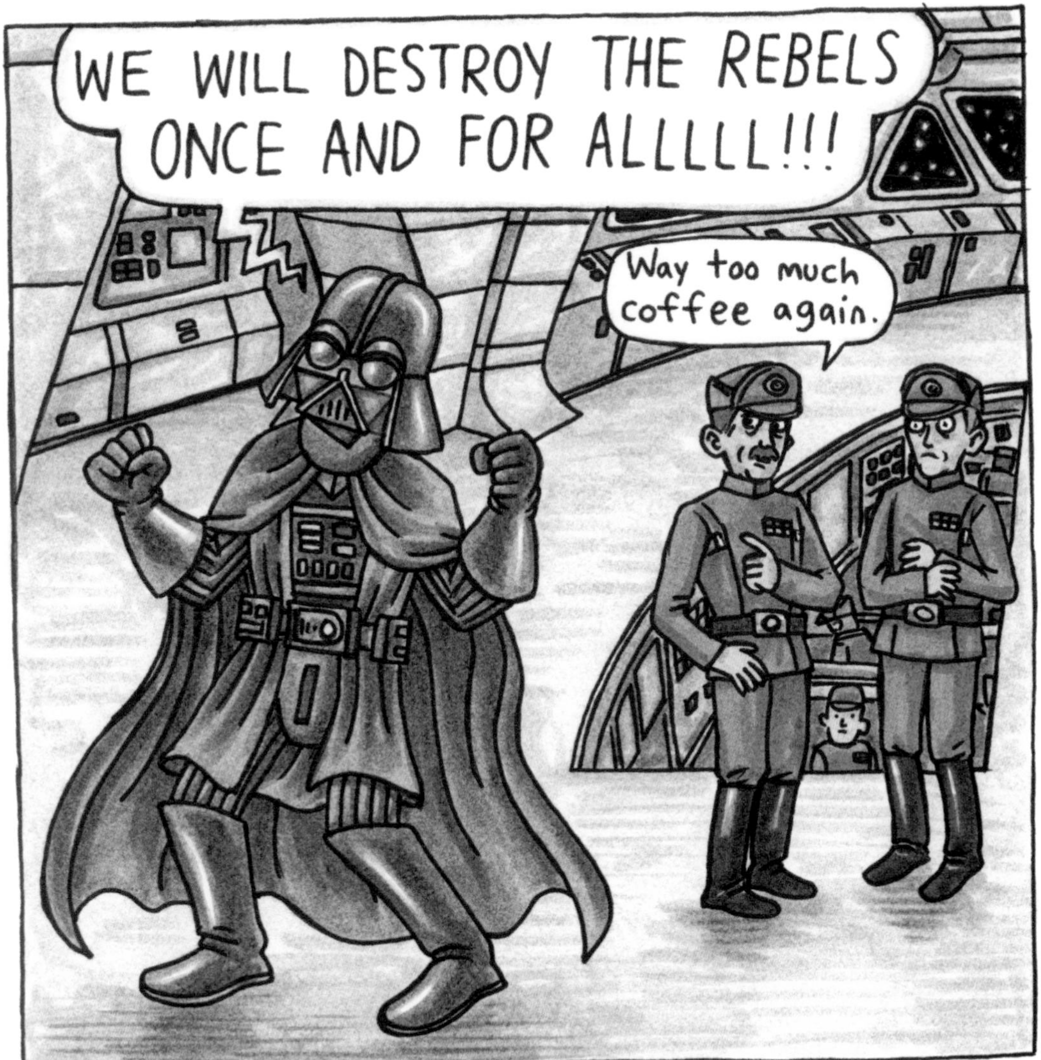
WE WILL DESTROY THE *REBELS* ONCE AND FOR ALLLLL!!!
Way too much coffee again.

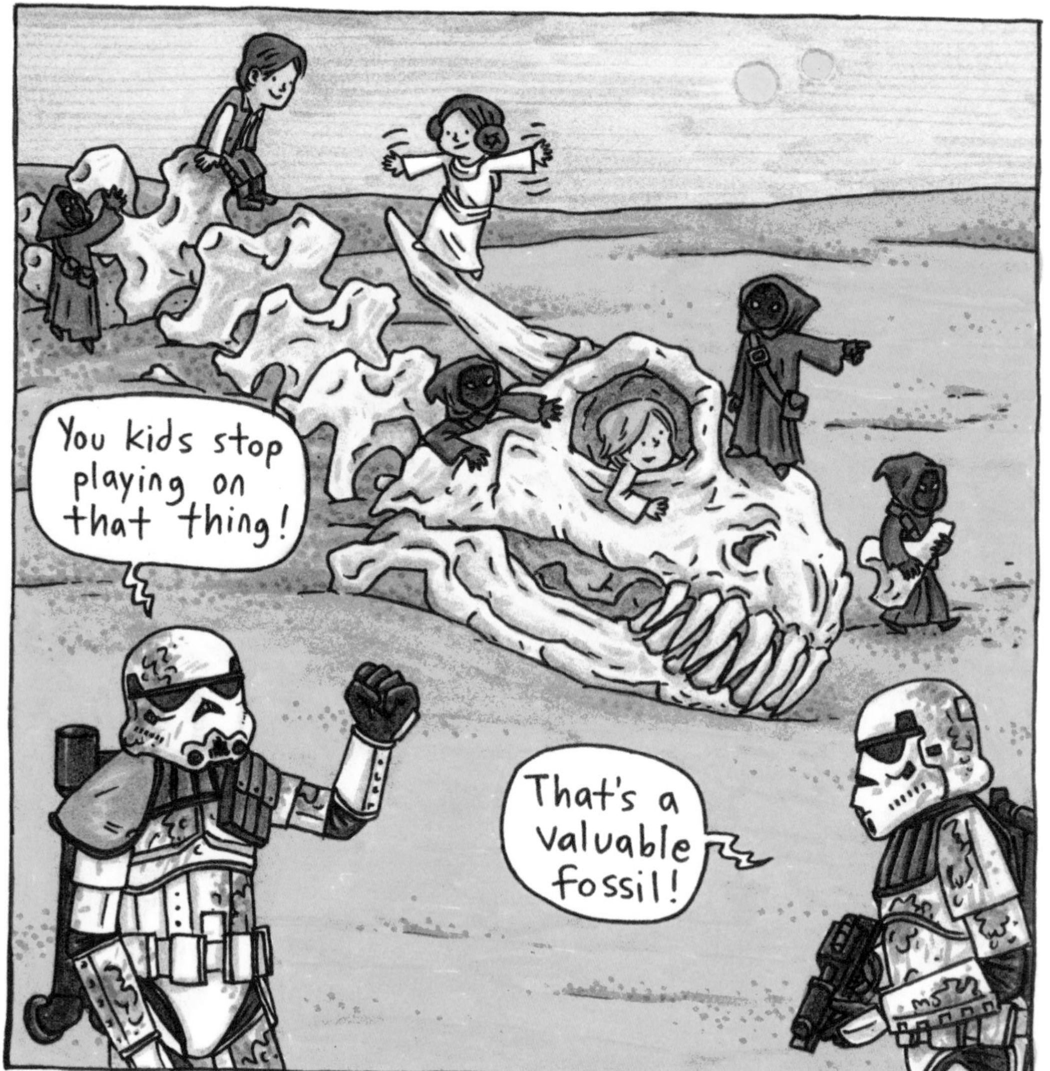
You kids stop playing on that thing!
That's a valuable fossil!

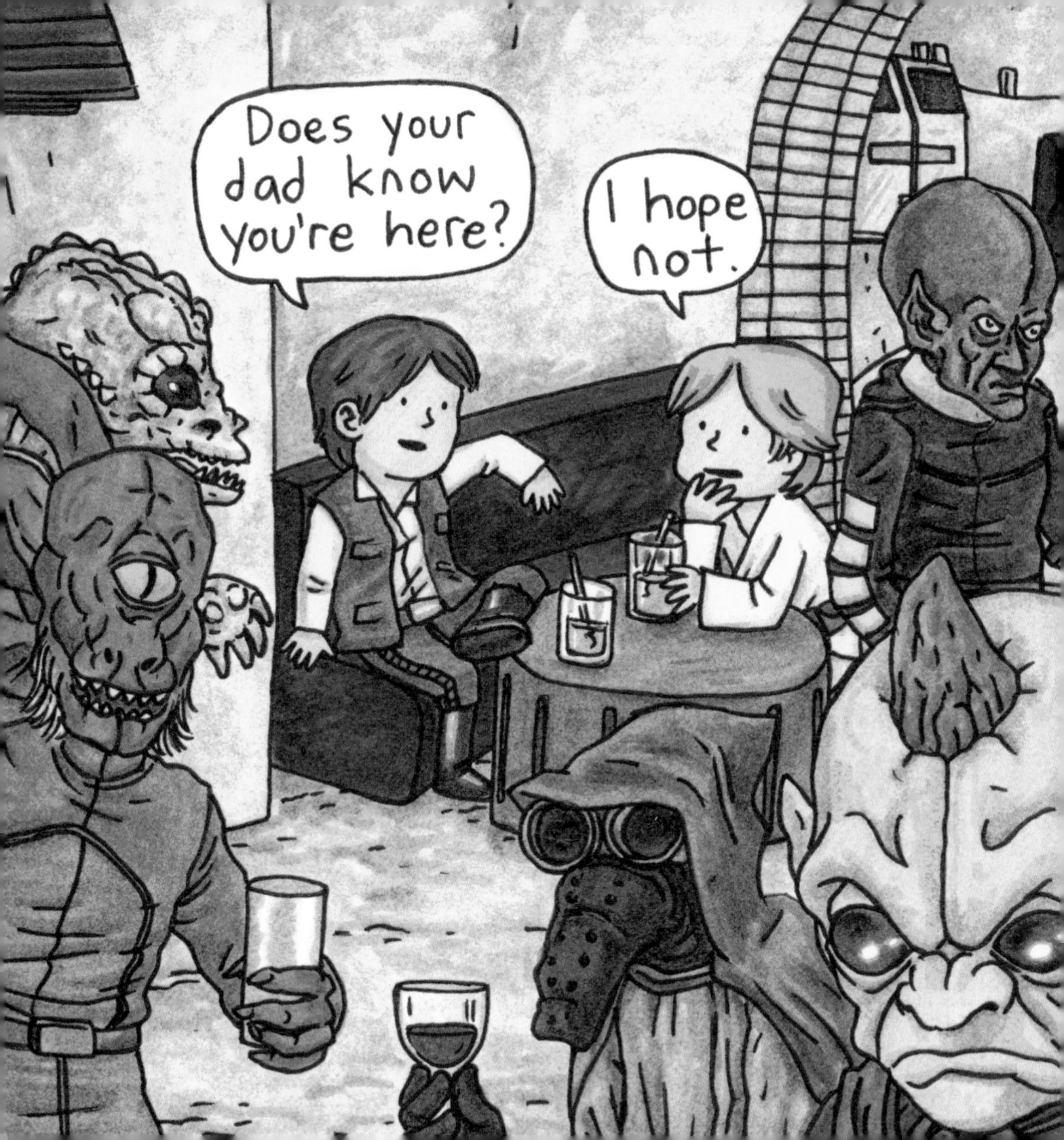
Does your dad know you're here?
I hope not.

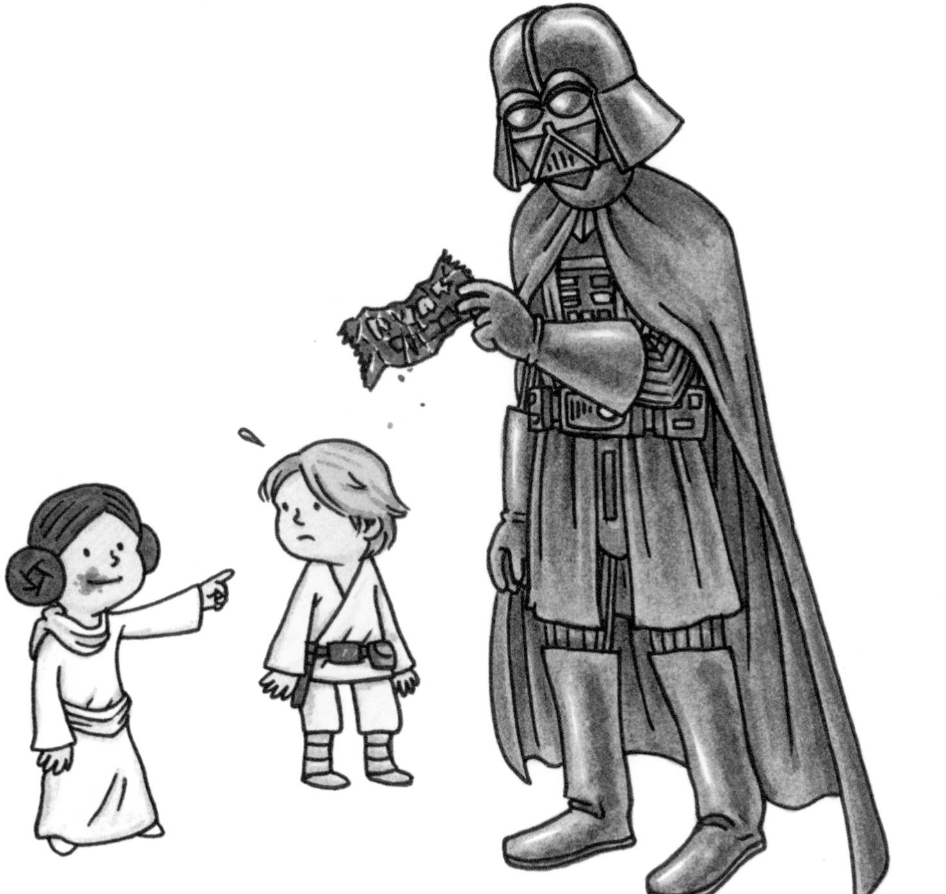

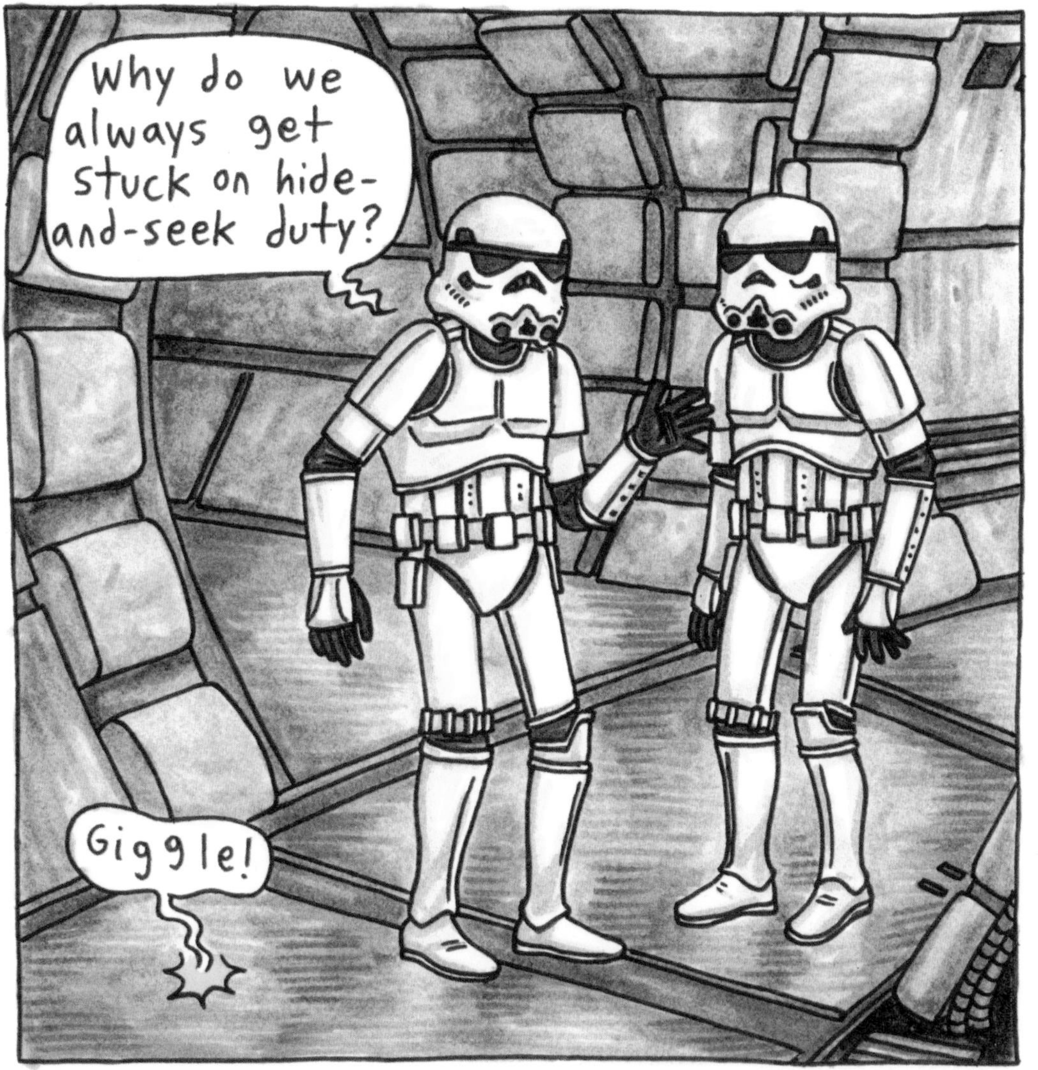
Why do we always get stuck on hide-and-seek duty?
Giggle!

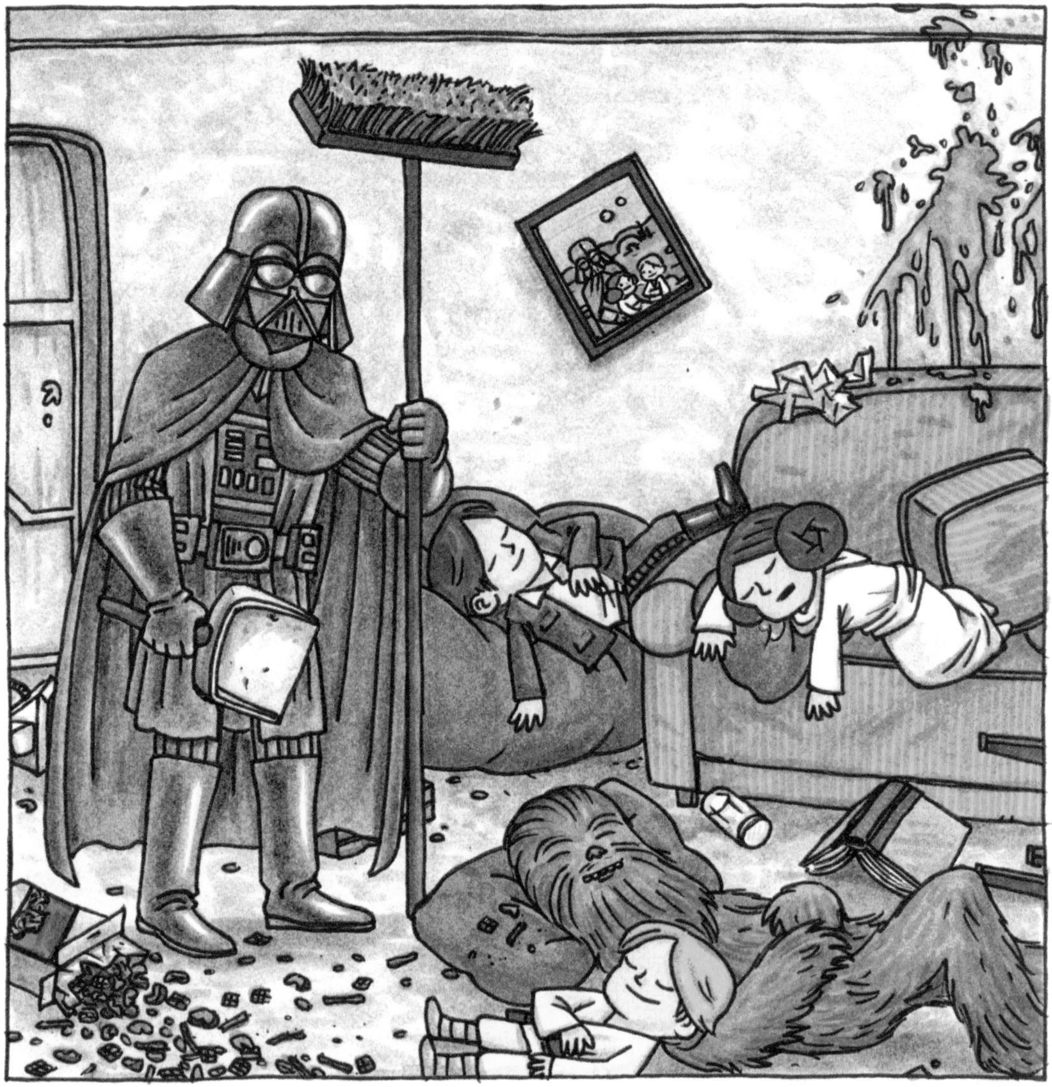

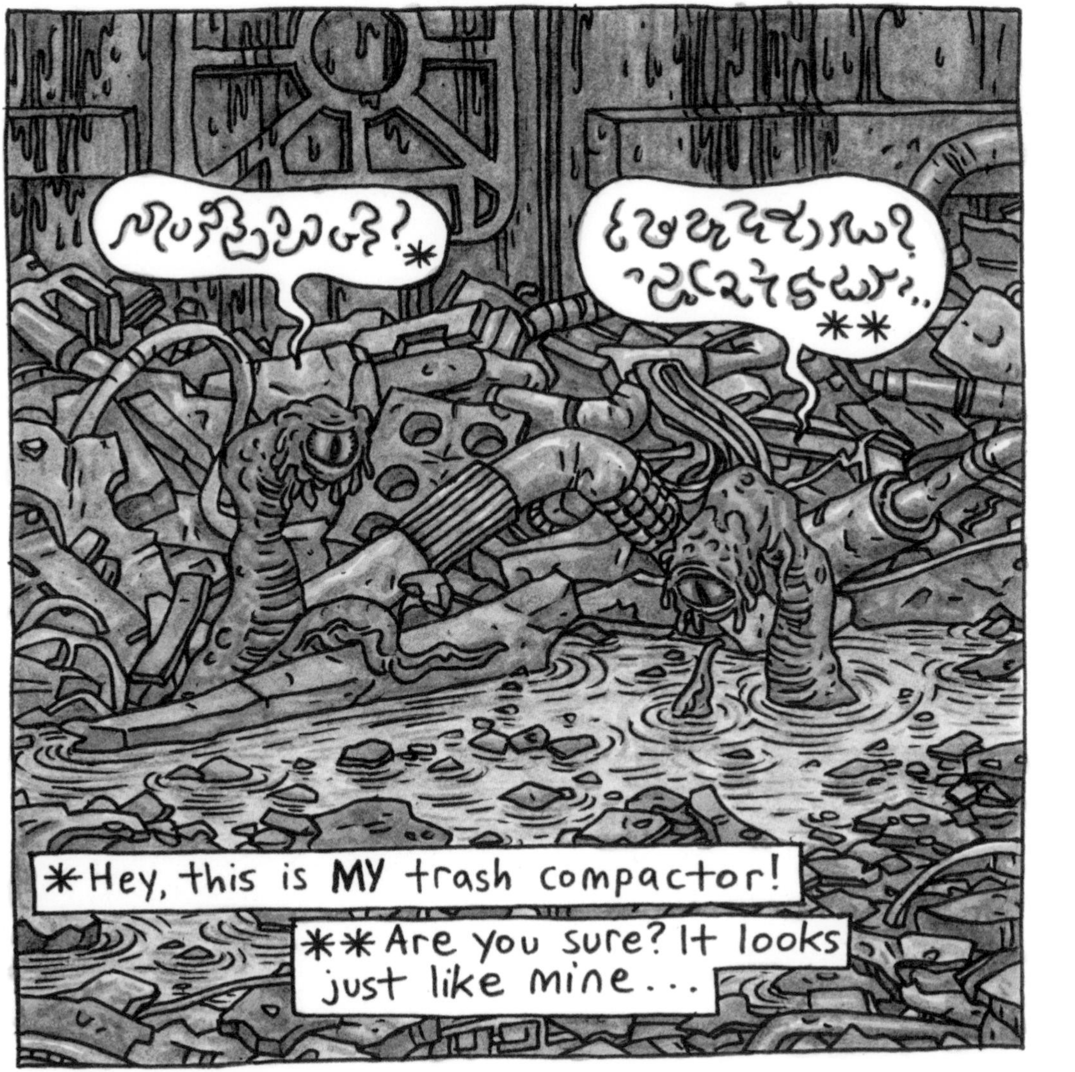
*Hey, this is MY trash compactor!
**Are you sure? It looks just like mine...

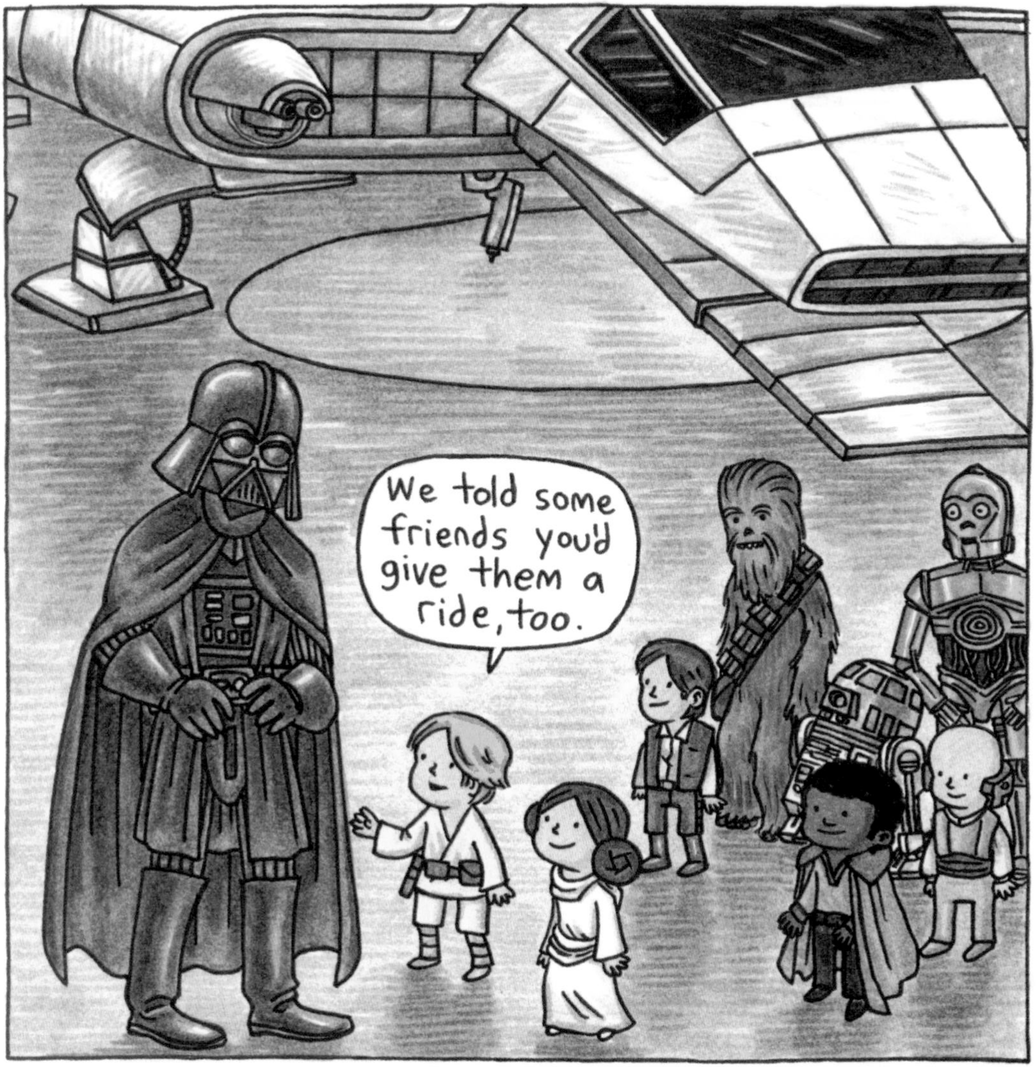
We told some friends you'd give them a ride, too.

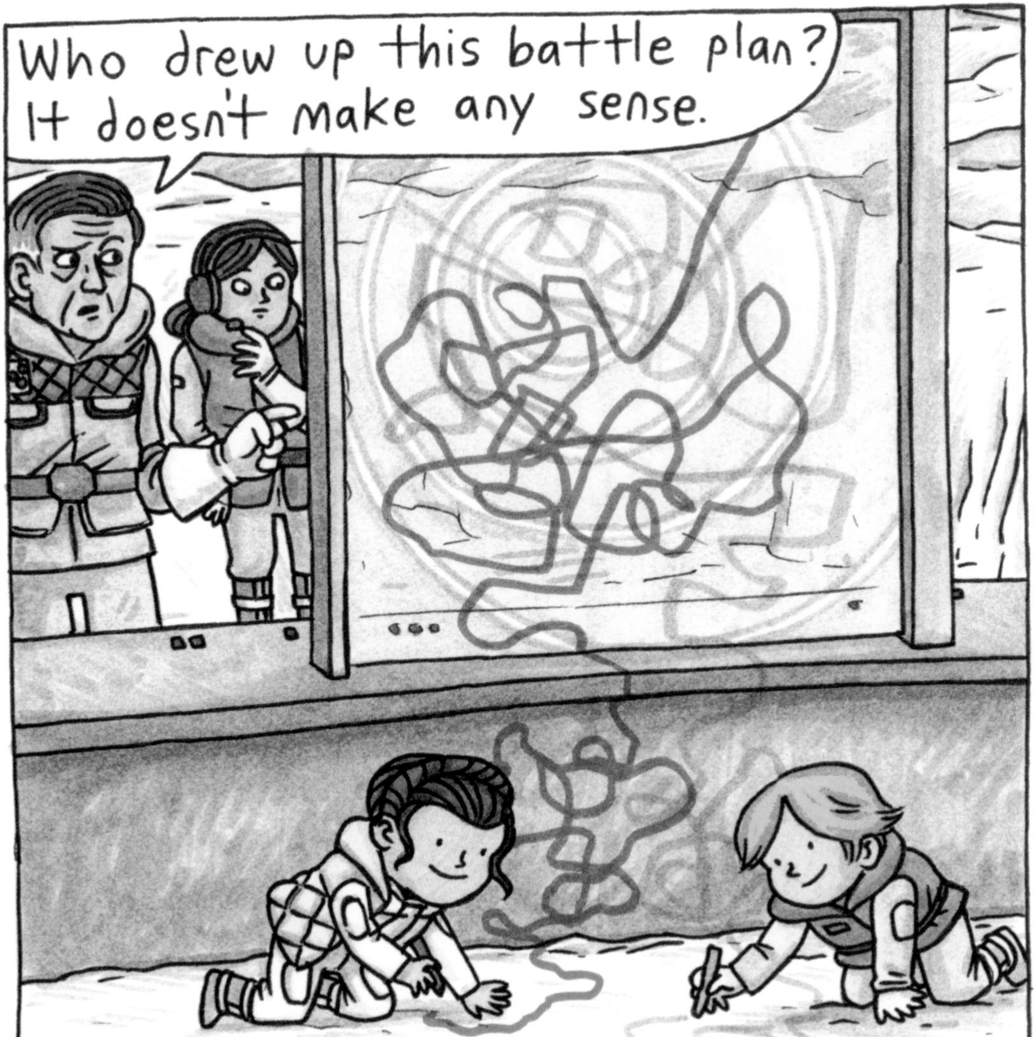
Who drew up this battle plan? It doesn't make any sense.

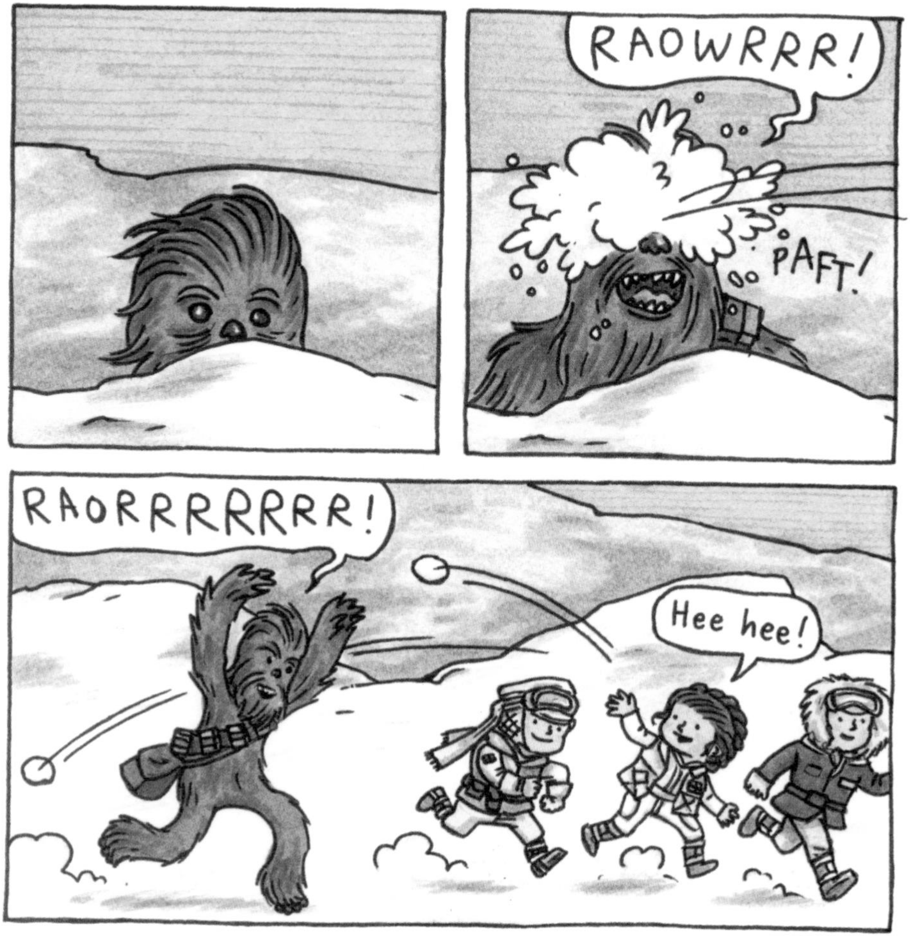
RAOWRRR!
PAFT!
RAORRRRRRR!
Hee hee!

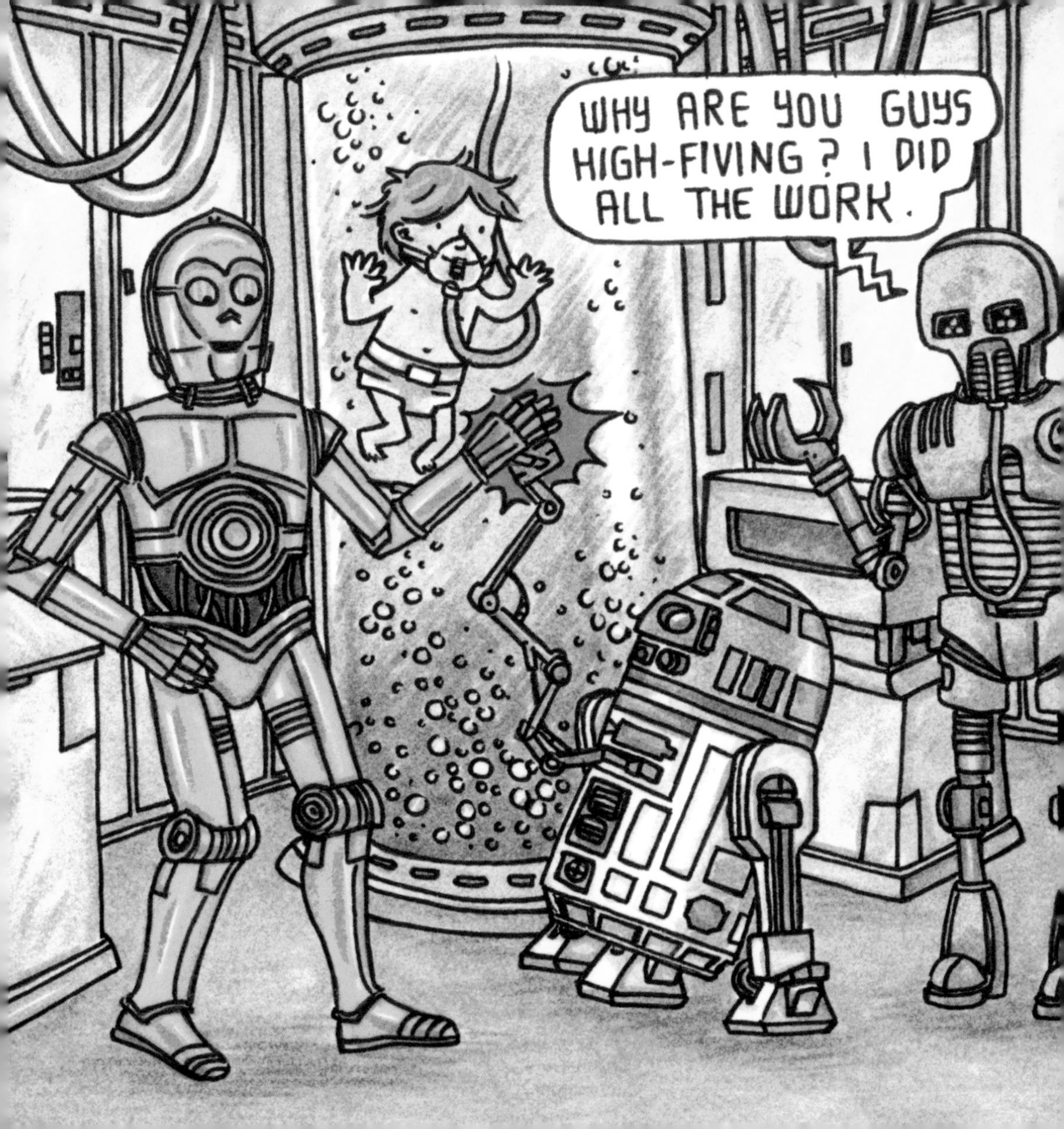
WHY ARE YOU GUYS HIGH-FIVING? I DID ALL THE WORK.

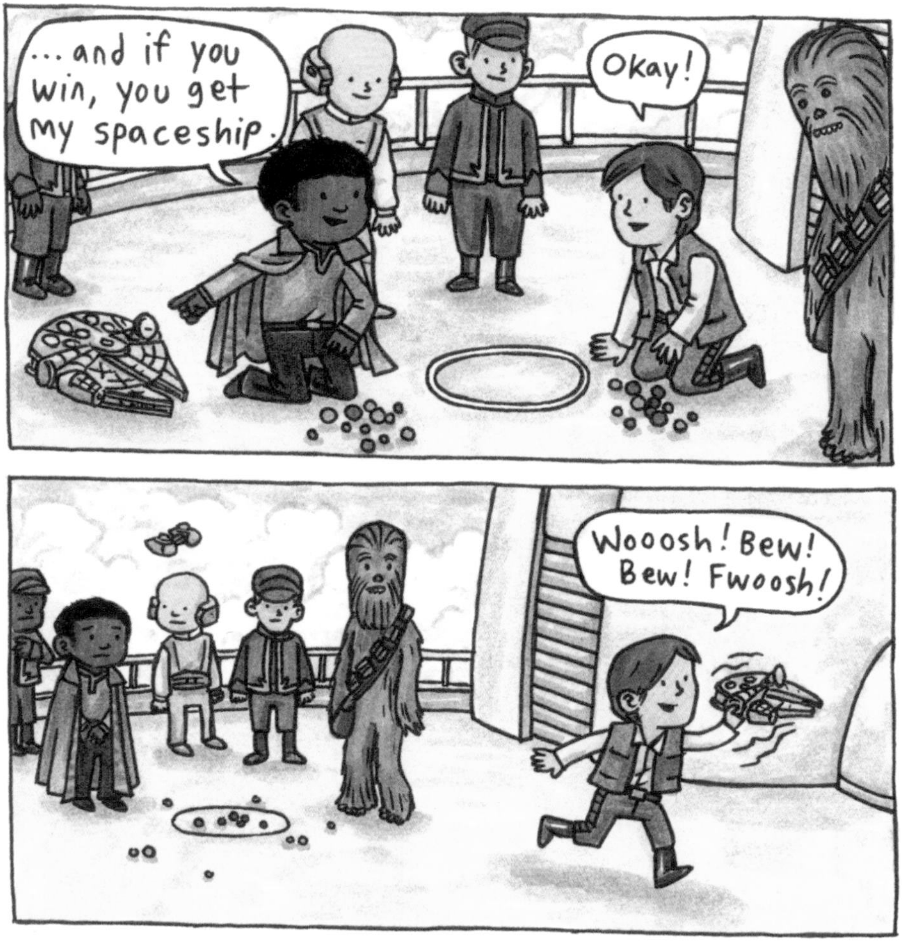
...and if you win, you get my spaceship.
Okay!
Wooosh! Bew! Bew! Fwoosh!

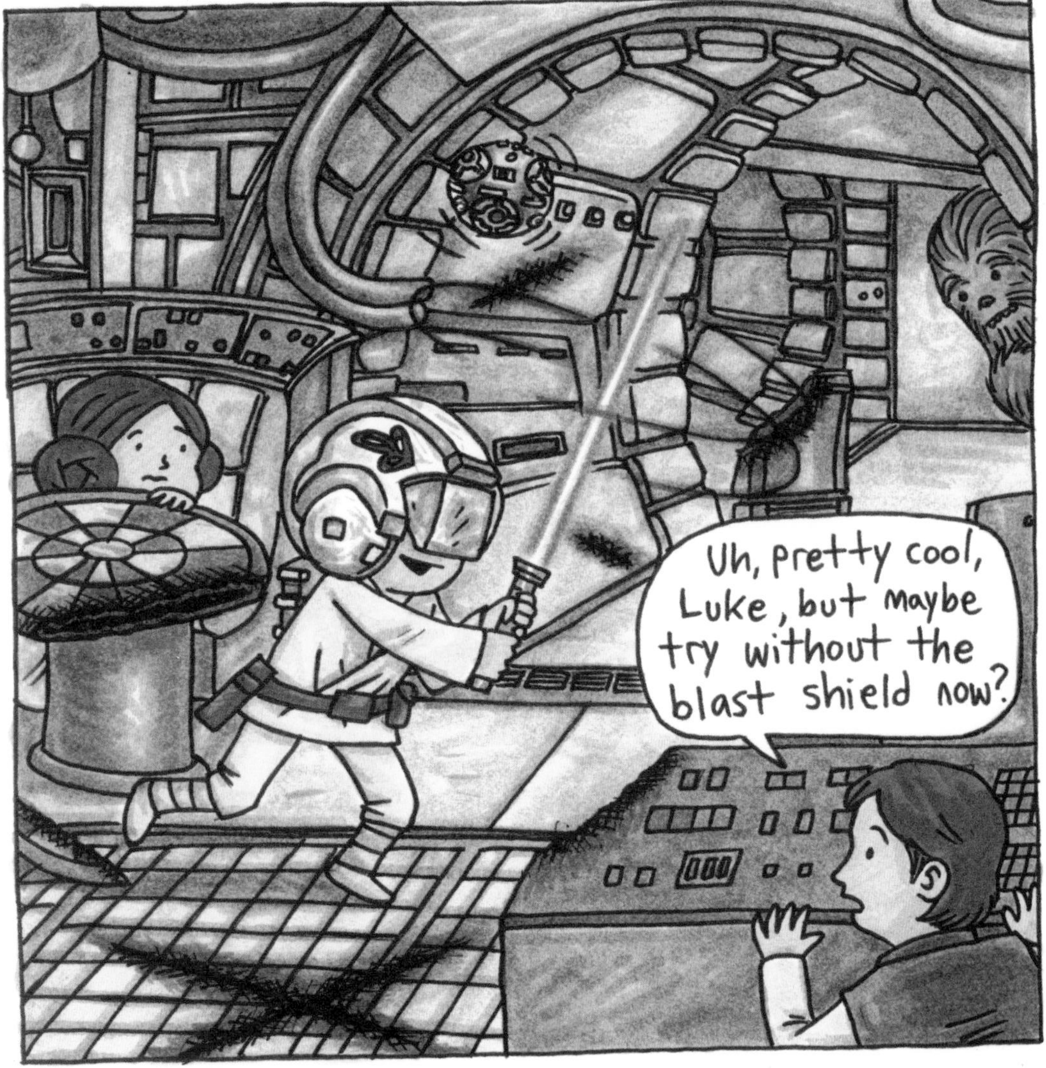
Uh, pretty cool, Luke, but maybe try without the blast shield now?

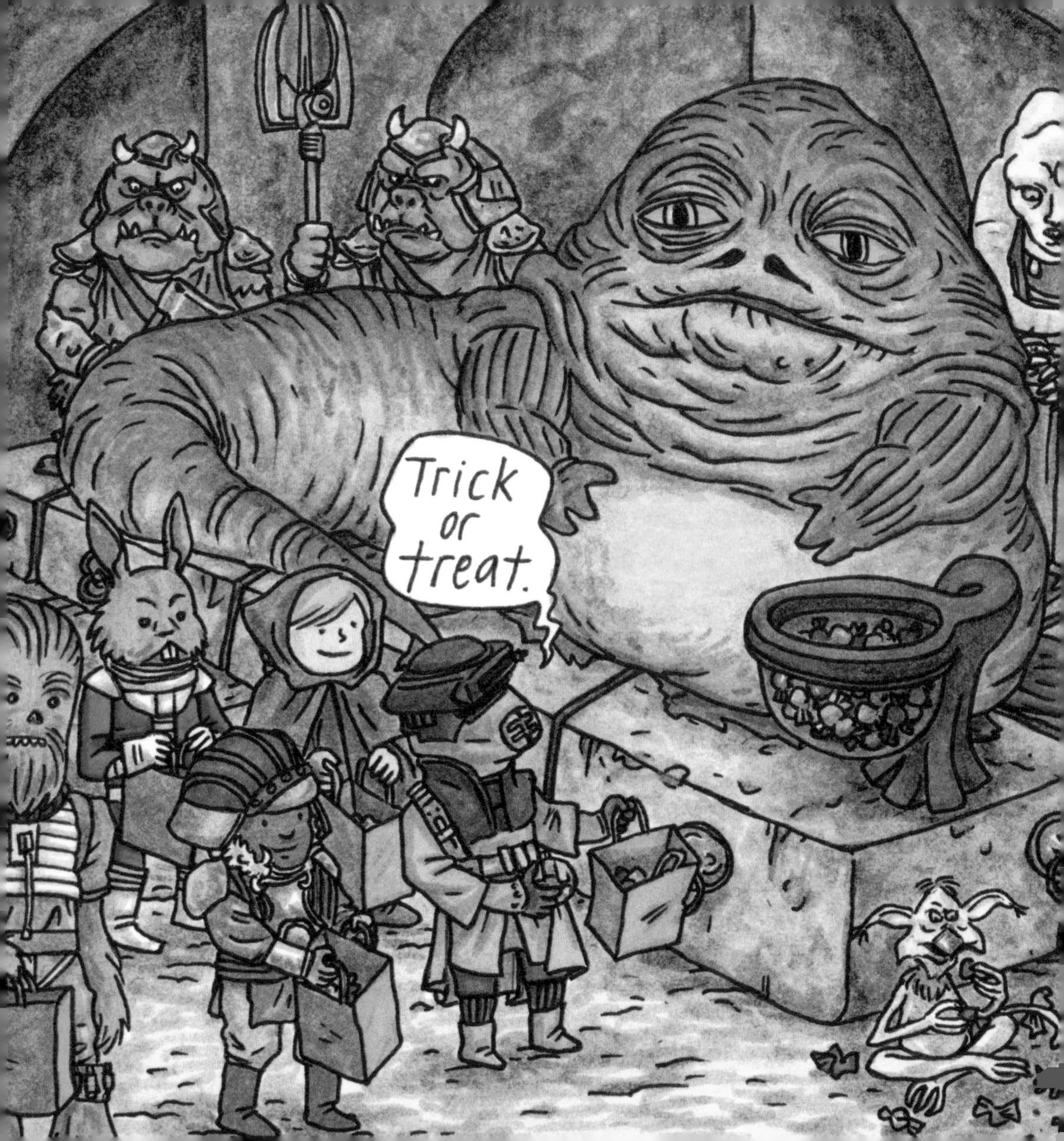
Trick or treat.

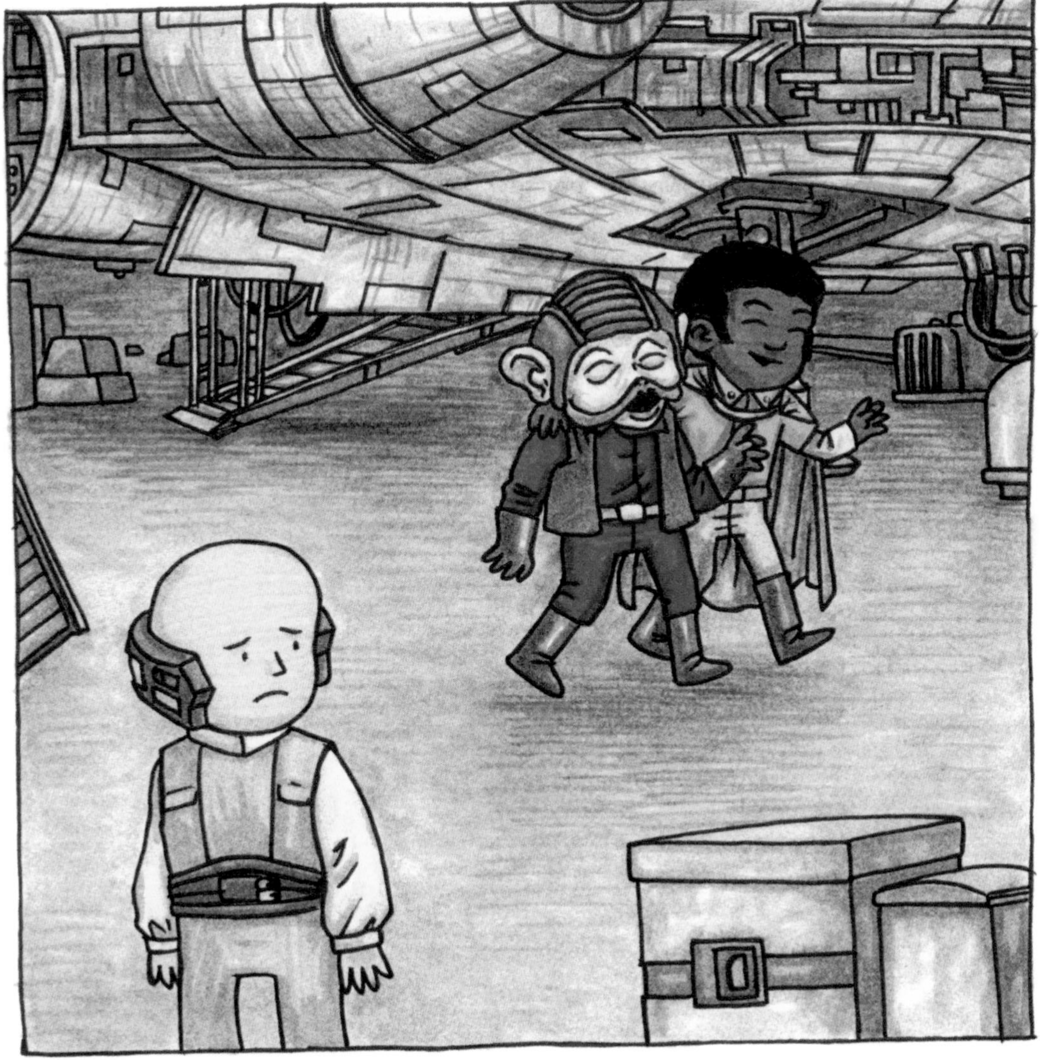

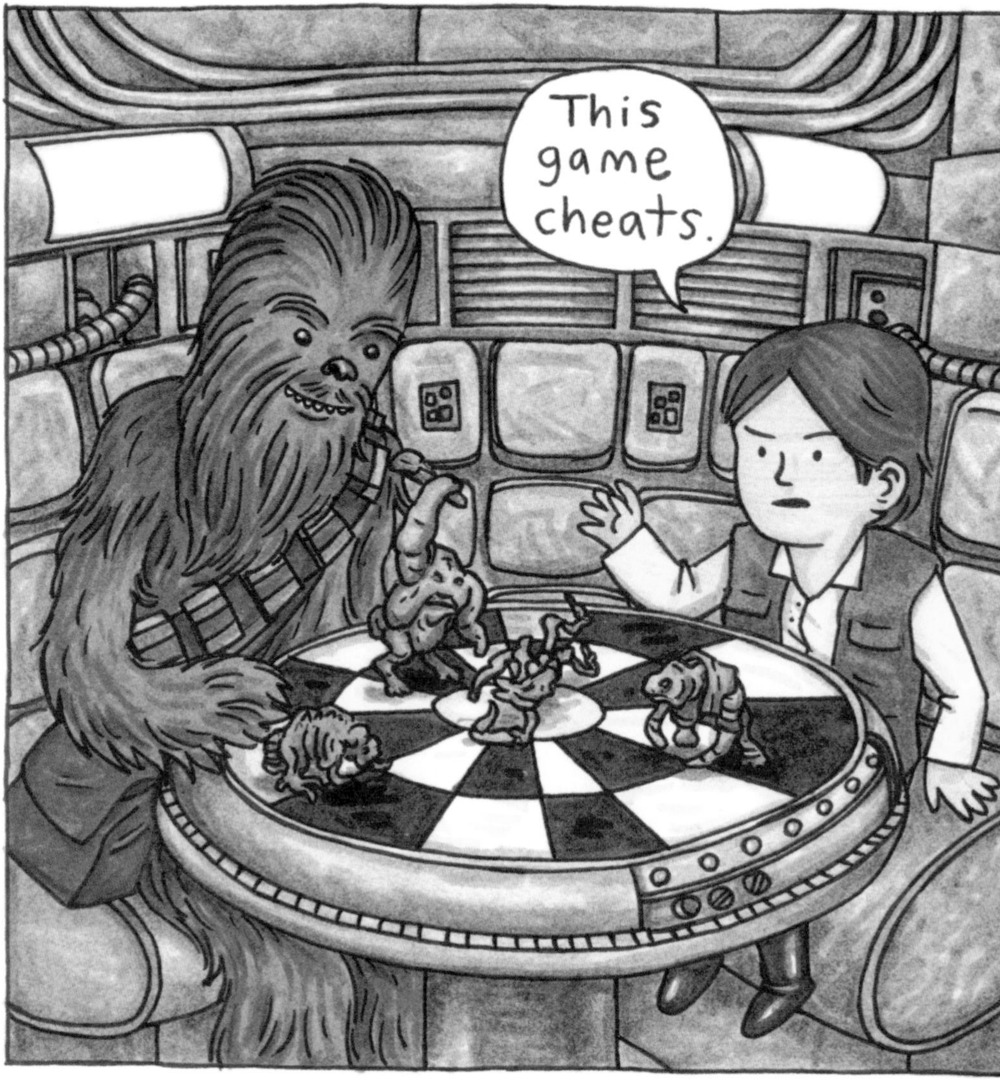
This game cheats.

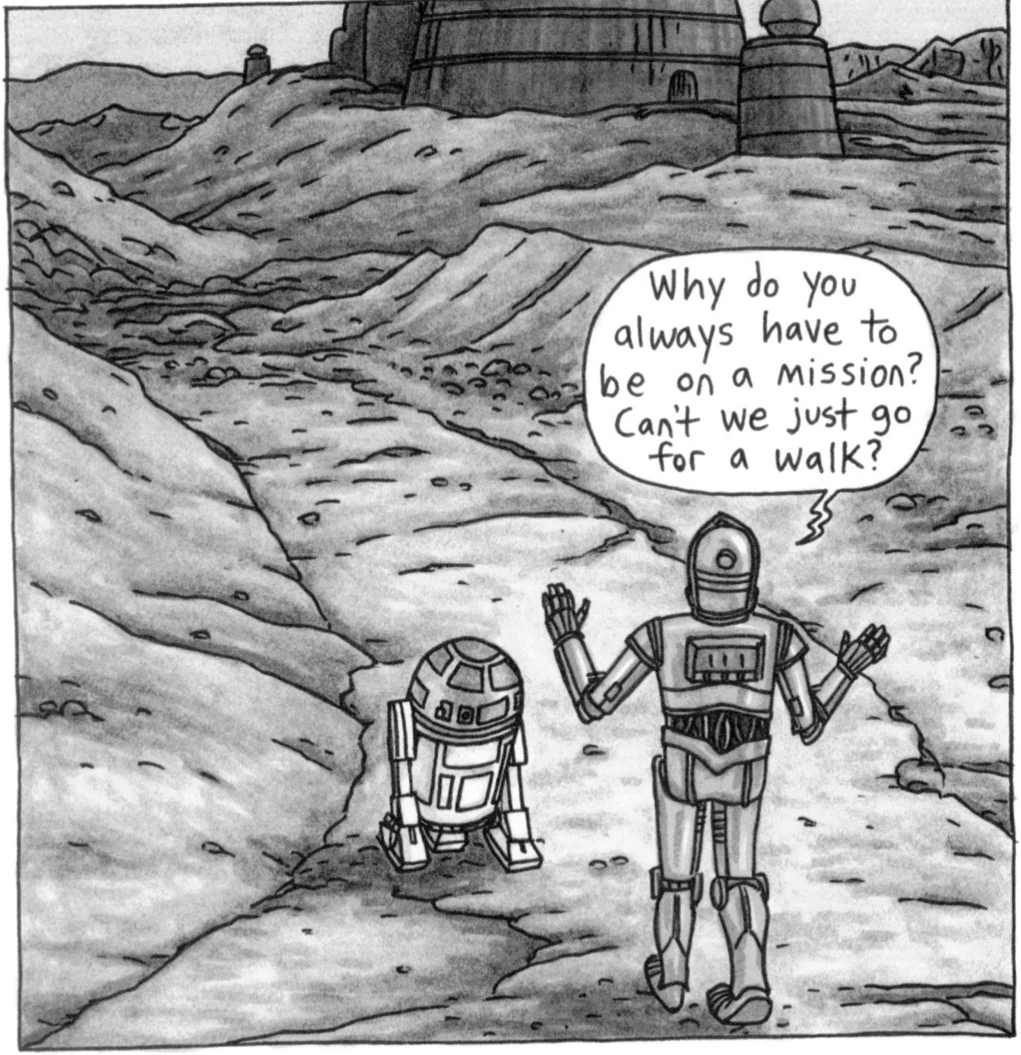
Why do you always have to be on a mission? Can't we just go for a walk?

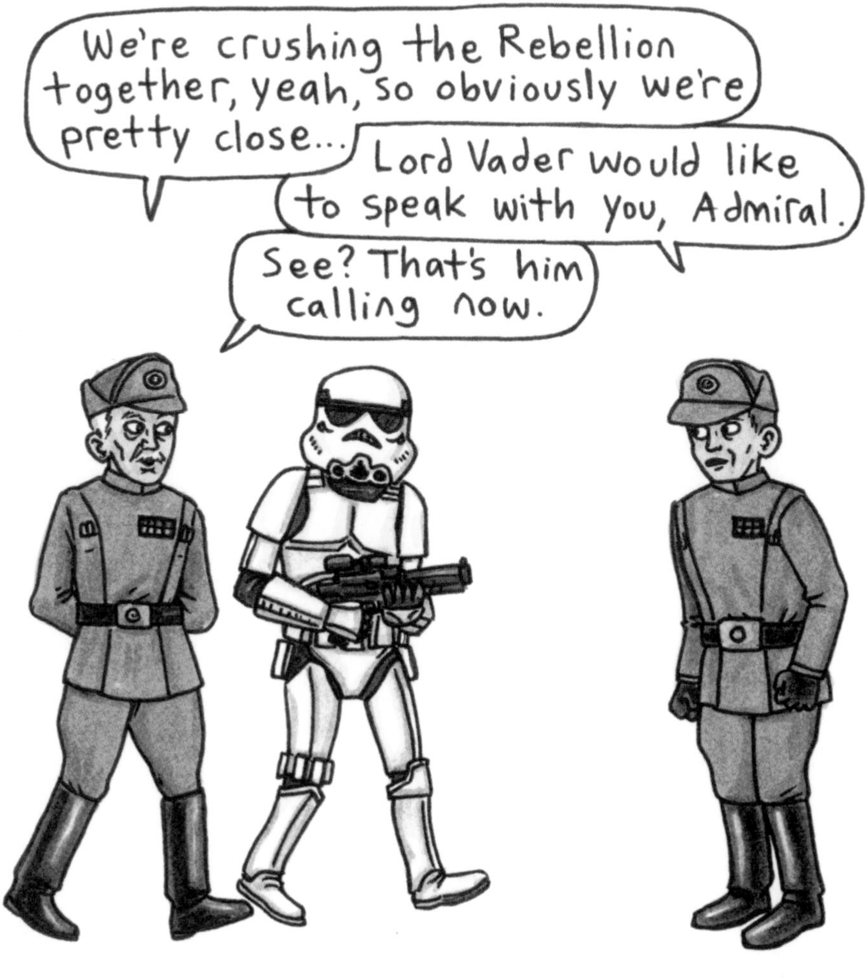
We're crushing the Rebellion together, yeah, so obviously we're pretty close...
Lord Vader would like to speak with you, Admiral.
See? That's him calling now.

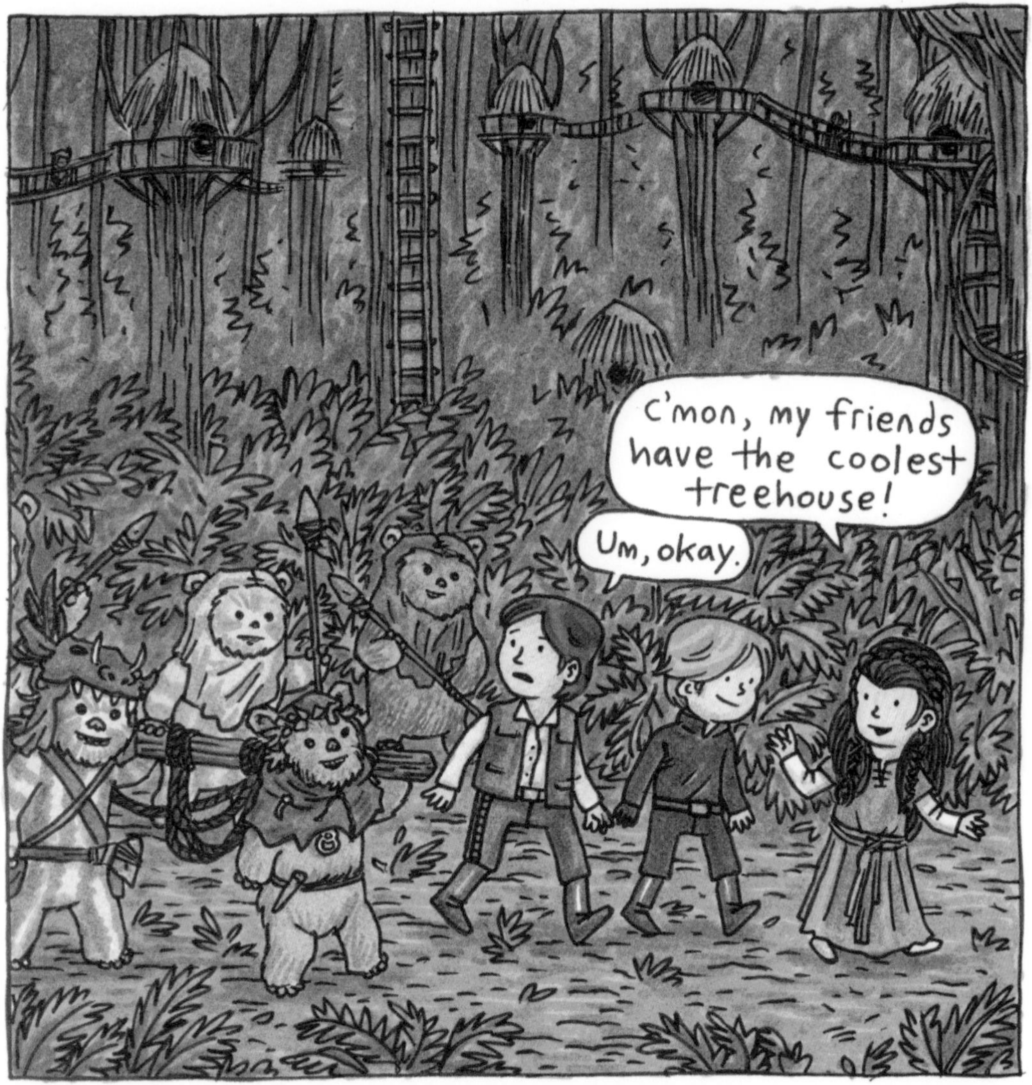
C'mon, my friends have the coolest treehouse!
Um, okay.

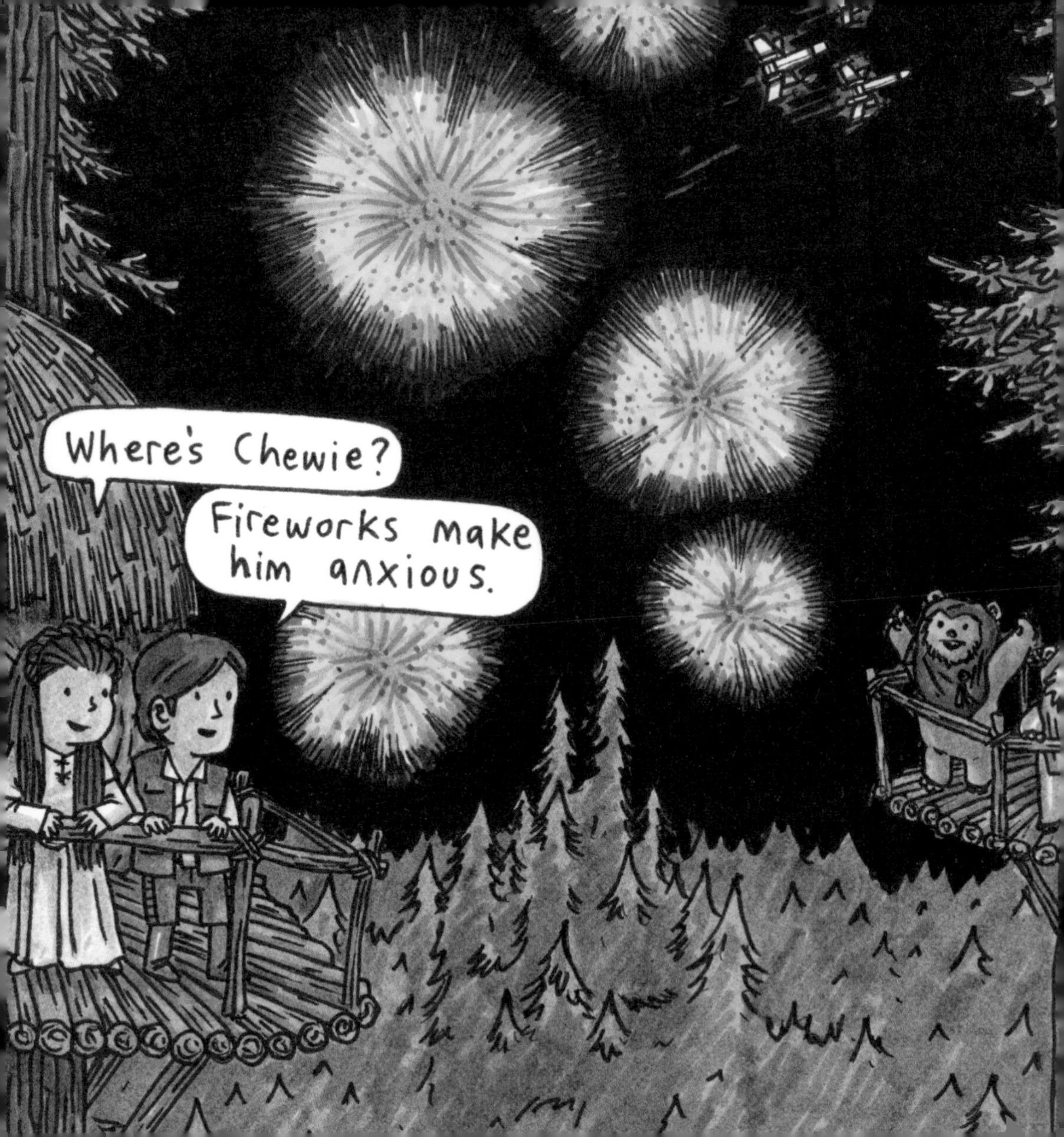
Where's Chewie?
Fireworks make him anxious.

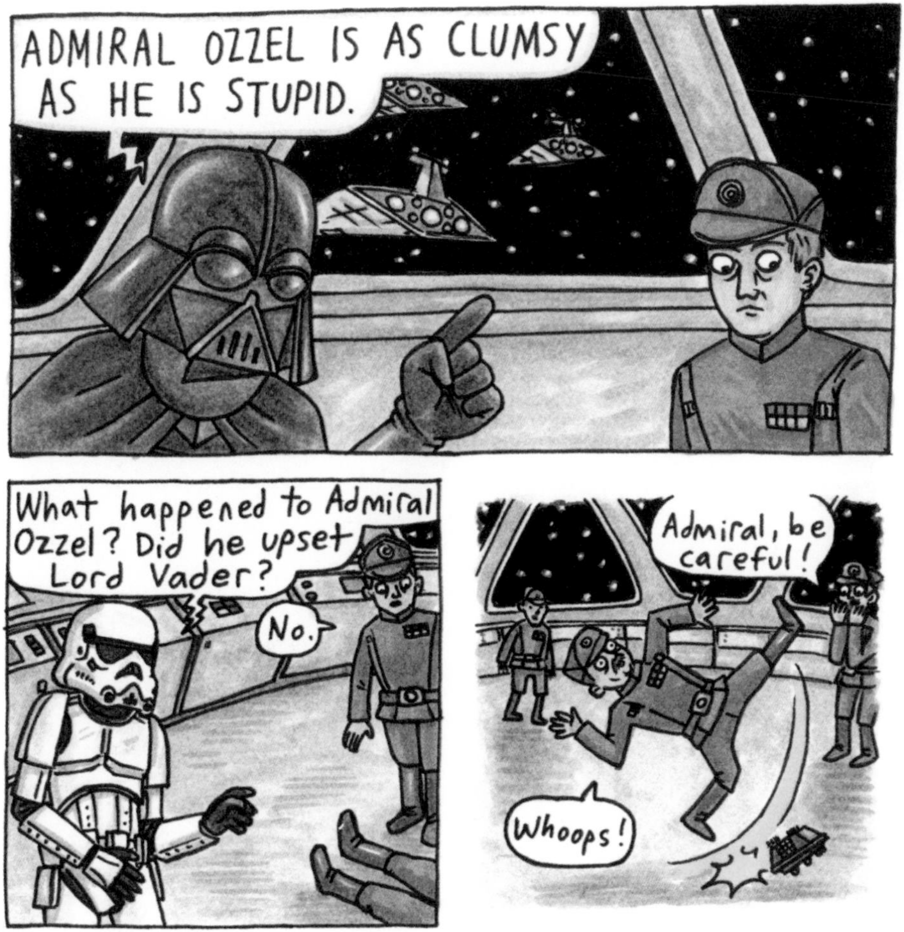
ADMIRAL OZZEL IS AS CLUMSY AS HE IS STUPID.
What happened to Admiral Ozzel? Did he upset Lord Vader?
No.
Admiral, be careful!
Whoops!

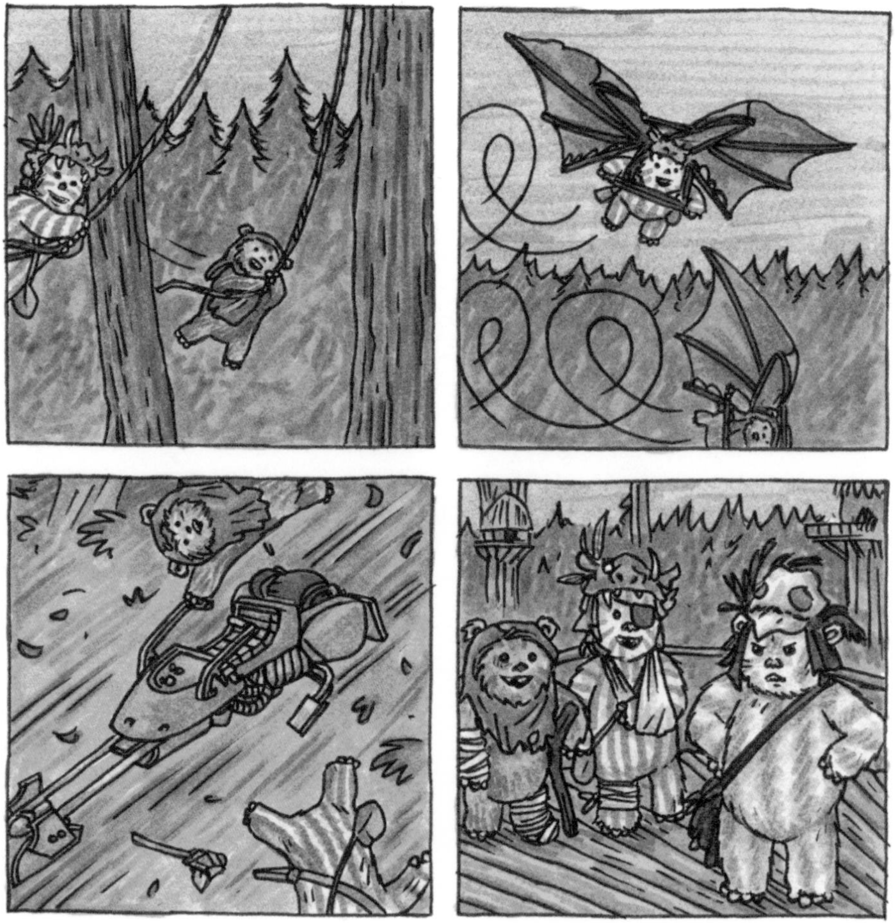

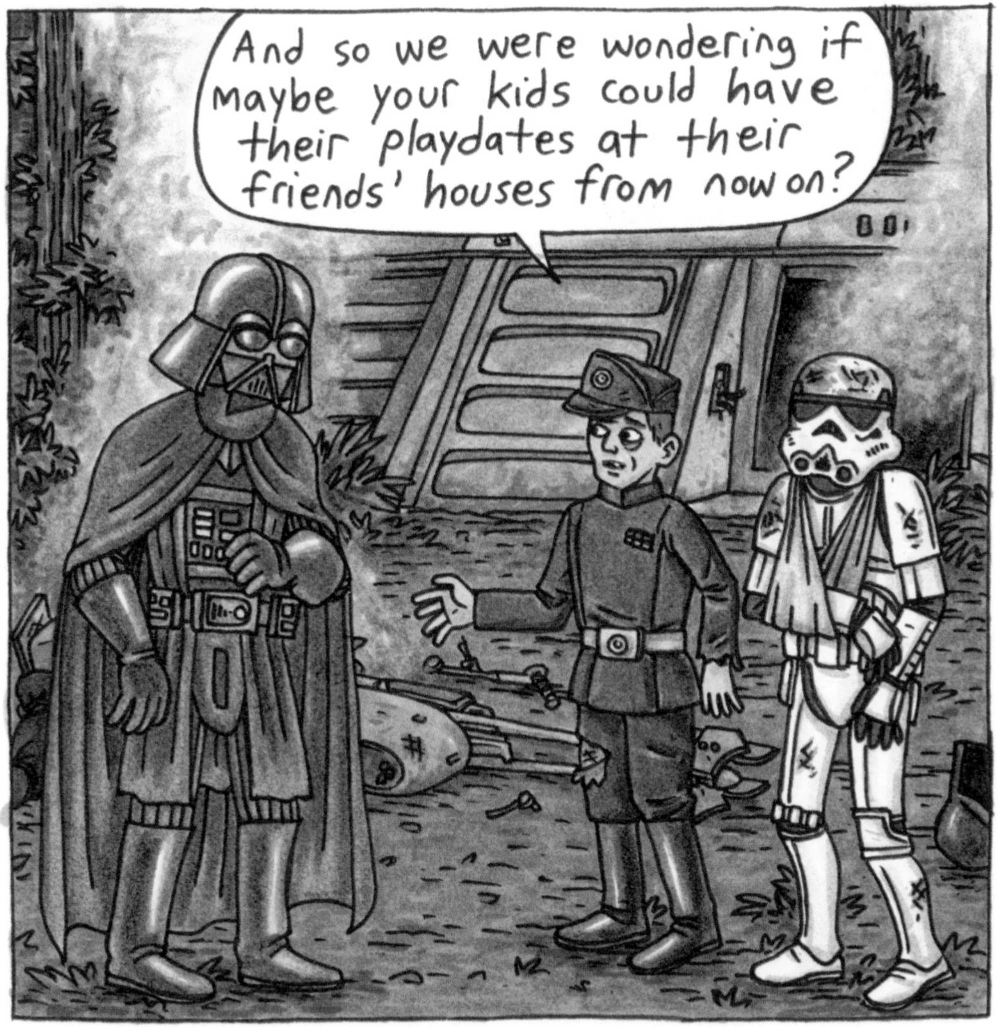
And so we were wondering if maybe your kids could have their playdates at their friends' houses from now on?

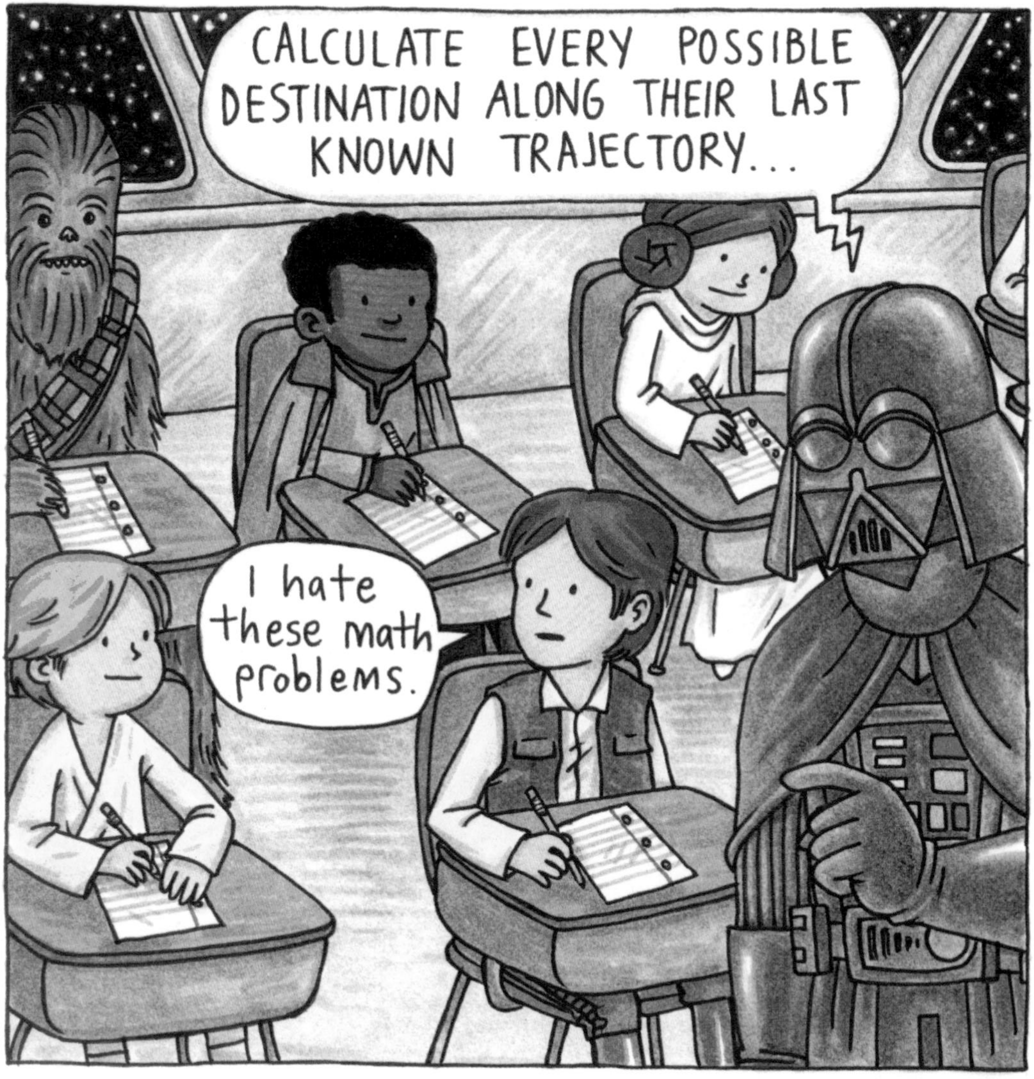
CALCULATE EVERY POSSIBLE DESTINATION ALONG THEIR LAST KNOWN TRAJECTORY...
I hate these math problems.

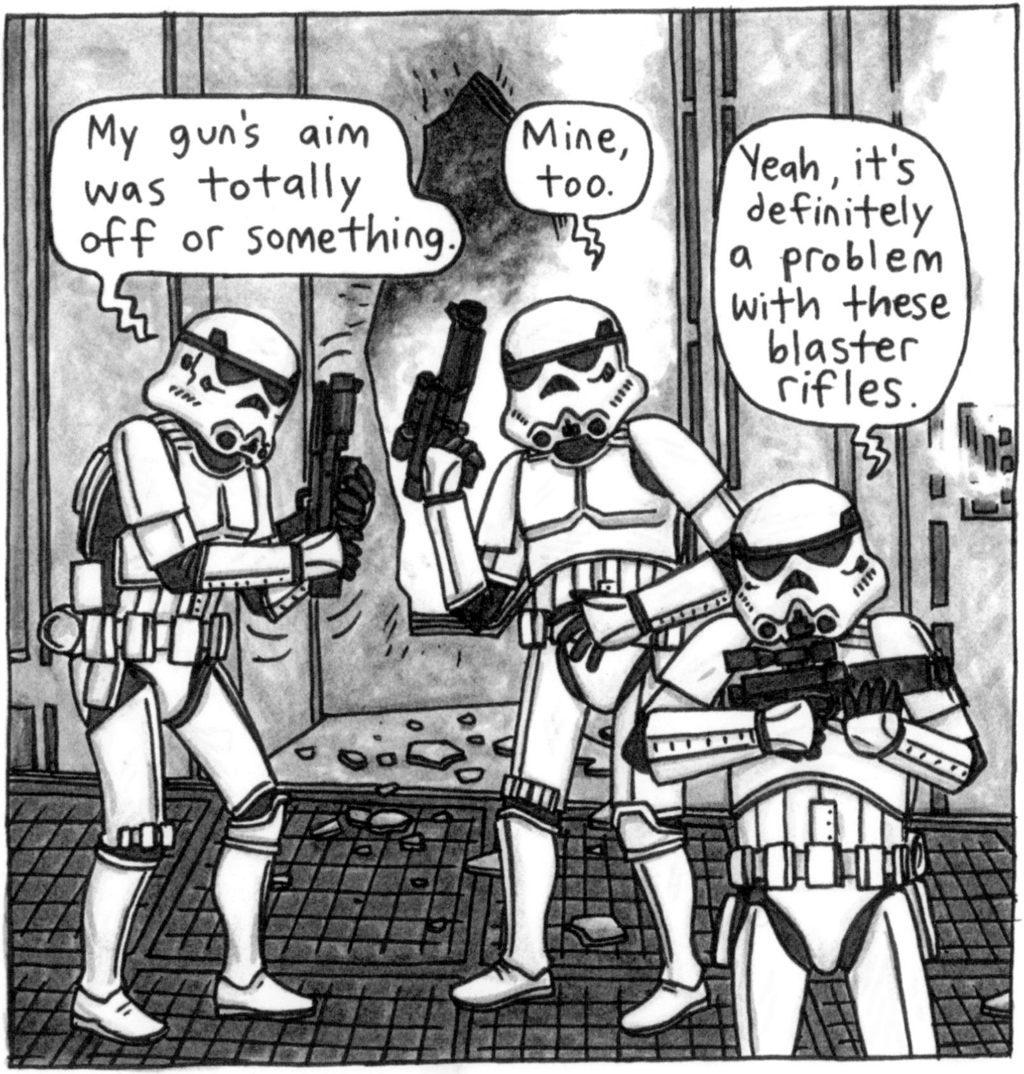
My gun's aim was totally off or something.
Mine, too.
Yeah, it's definitely a problem with these blaster rifles.

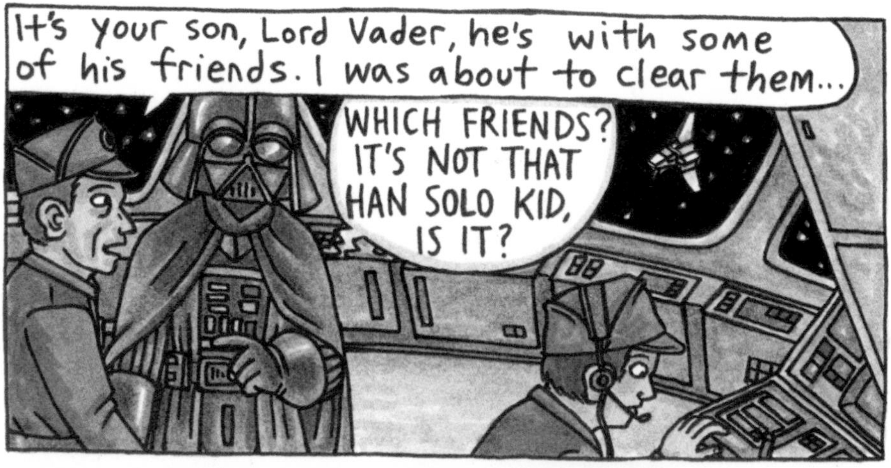
It's your son, Lord Vader, he's with some of his friends. I was about to clear them...
WHICH FRIENDS? IT'S NOT THAT HAN SOLO KID, IS IT?

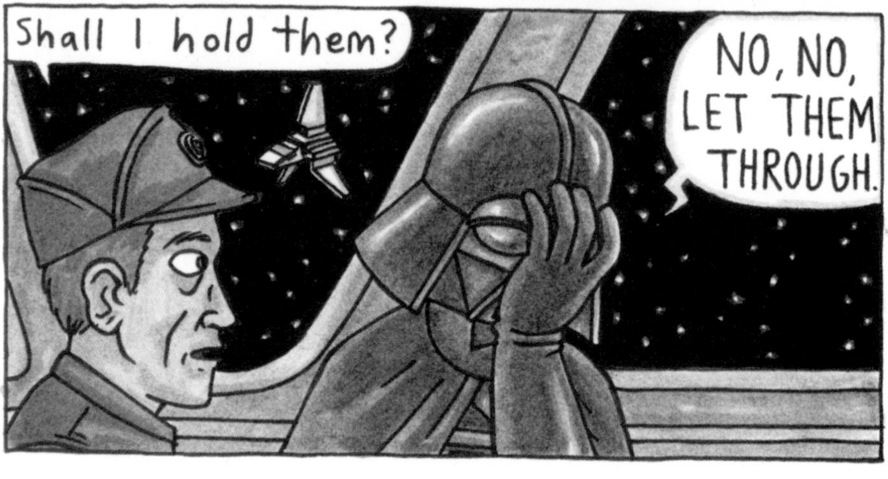
Shall I hold them?
NO, NO, LET THEM THROUGH.

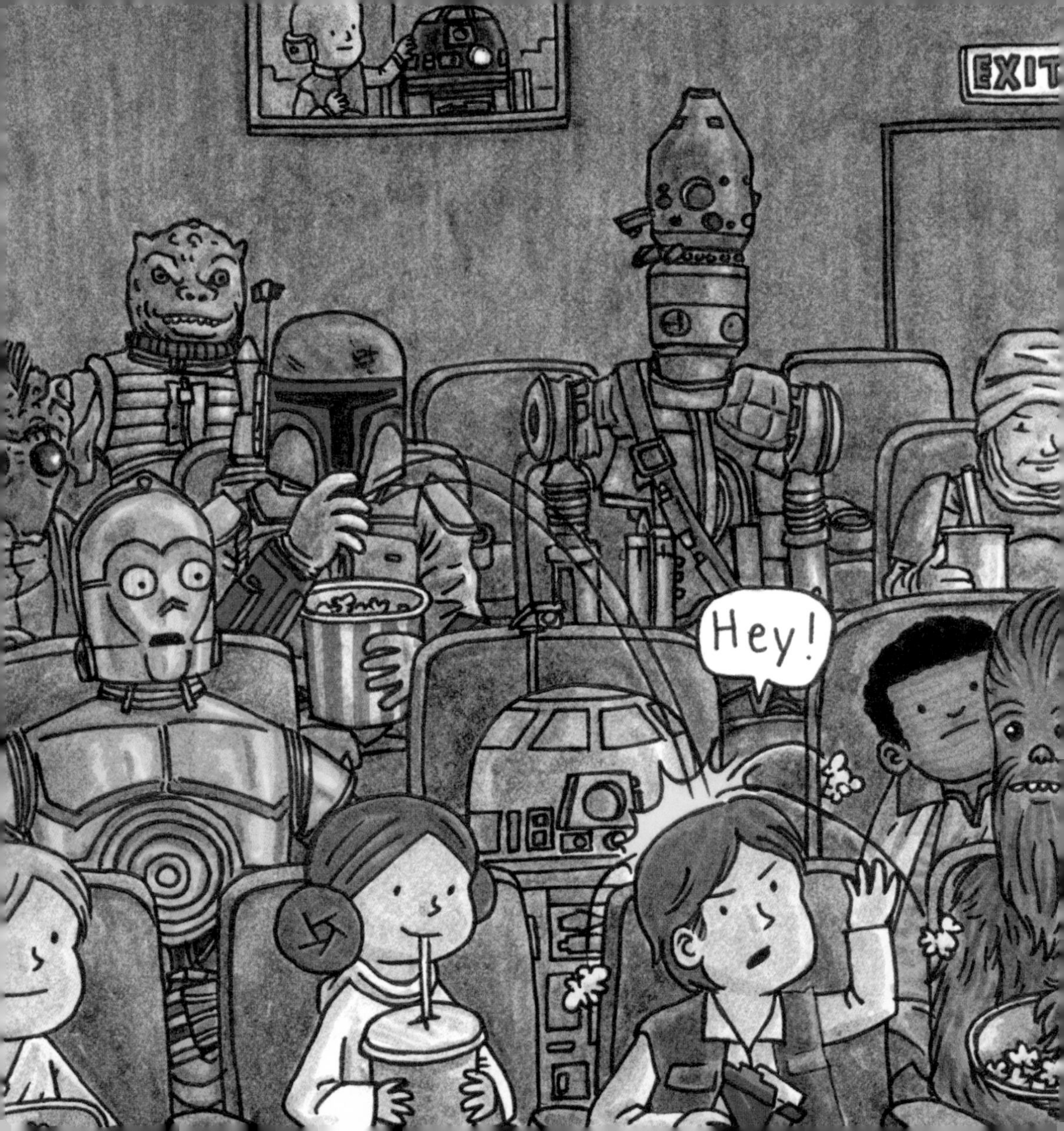
EXIT
Hey!

You wouldn't REALLY kiss her, would you?

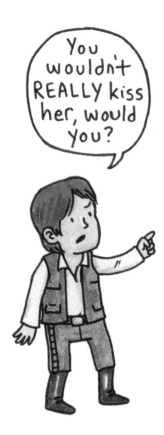

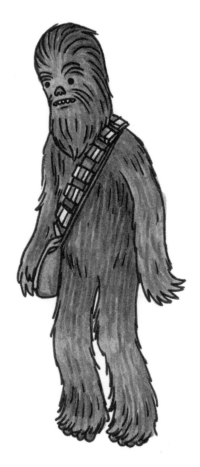

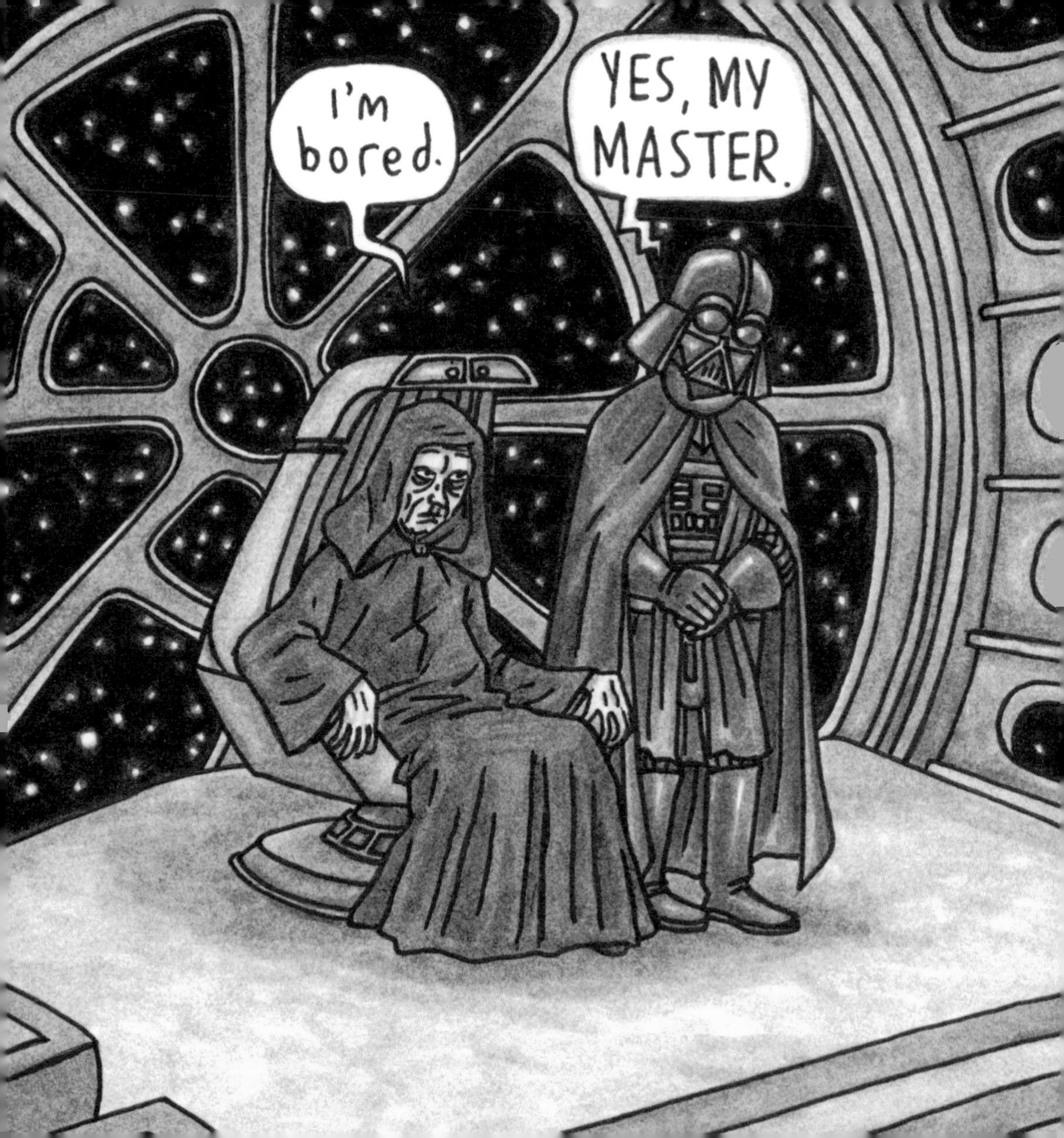
I'm bored.
YES, MY MASTER.

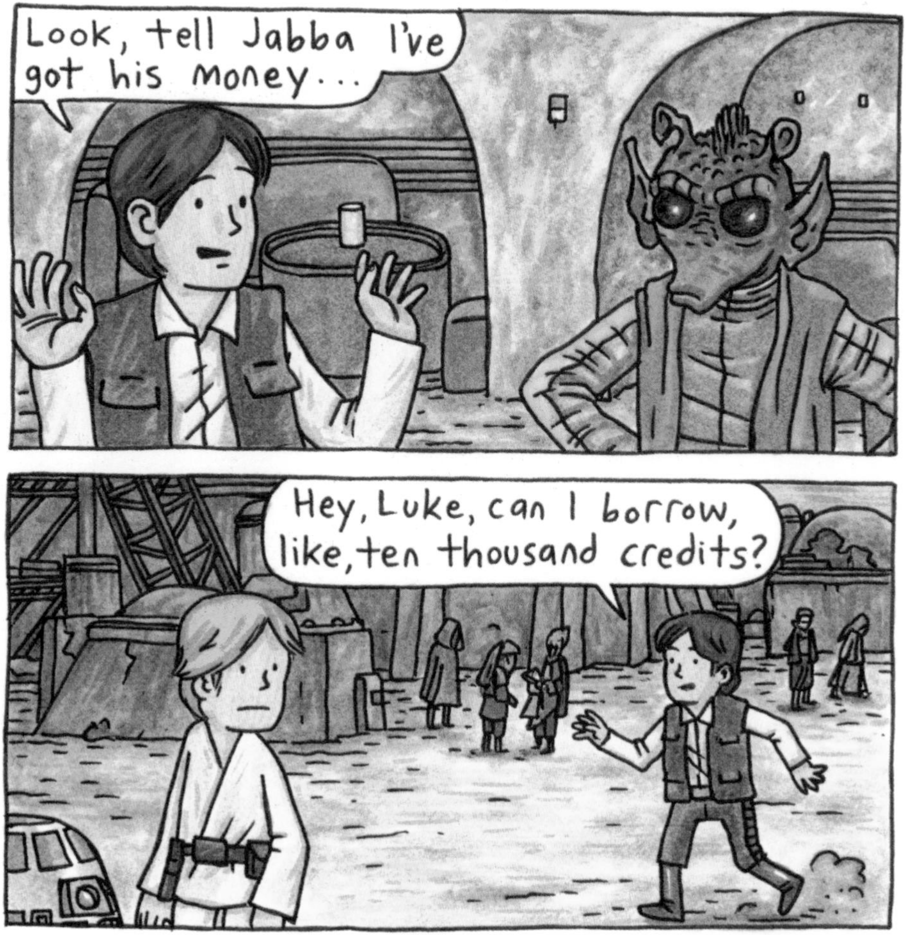
Look, tell Jabba I've got his money...
Hey, Luke, can I borrow, like, ten thousand credits?

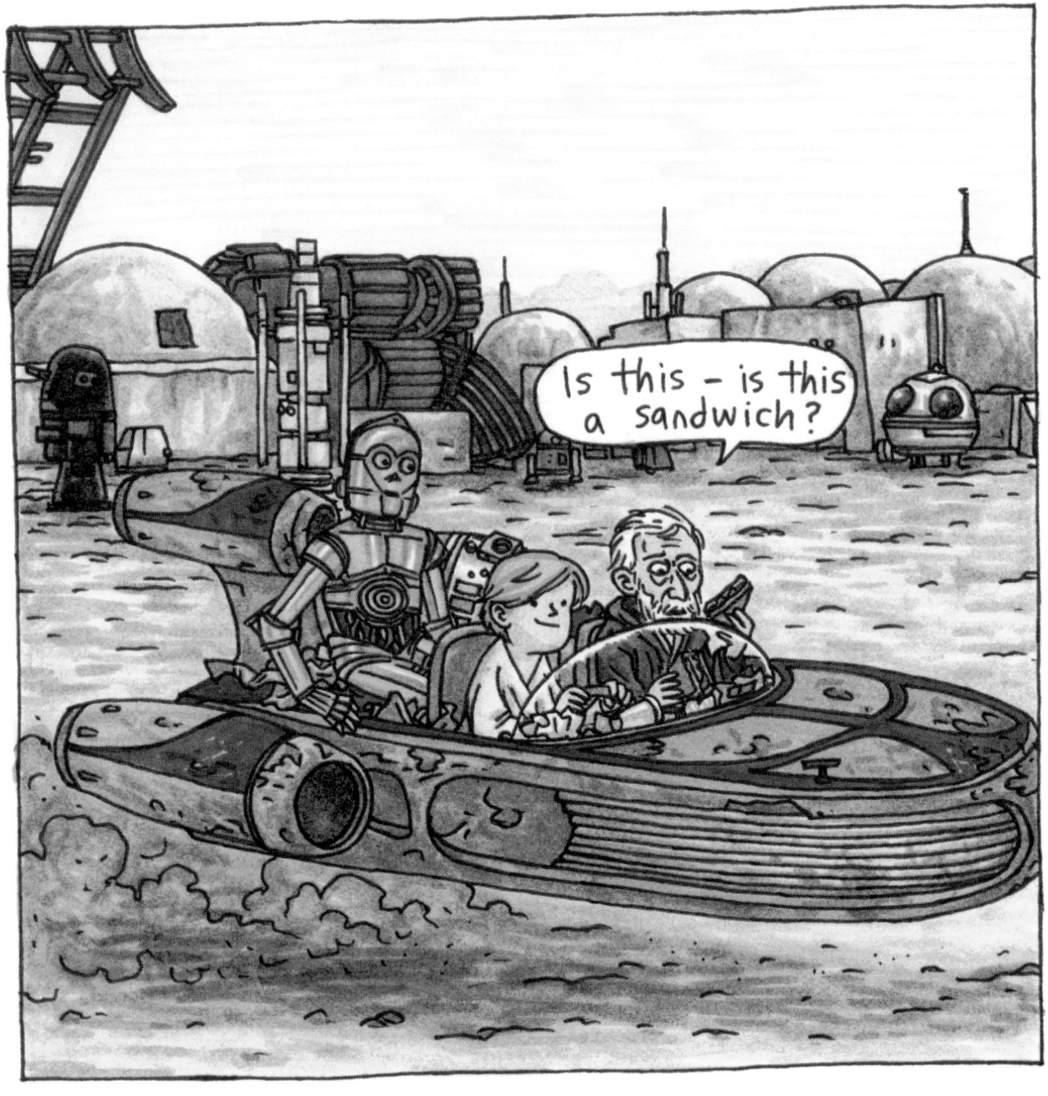
Is this - is this a sandwich?

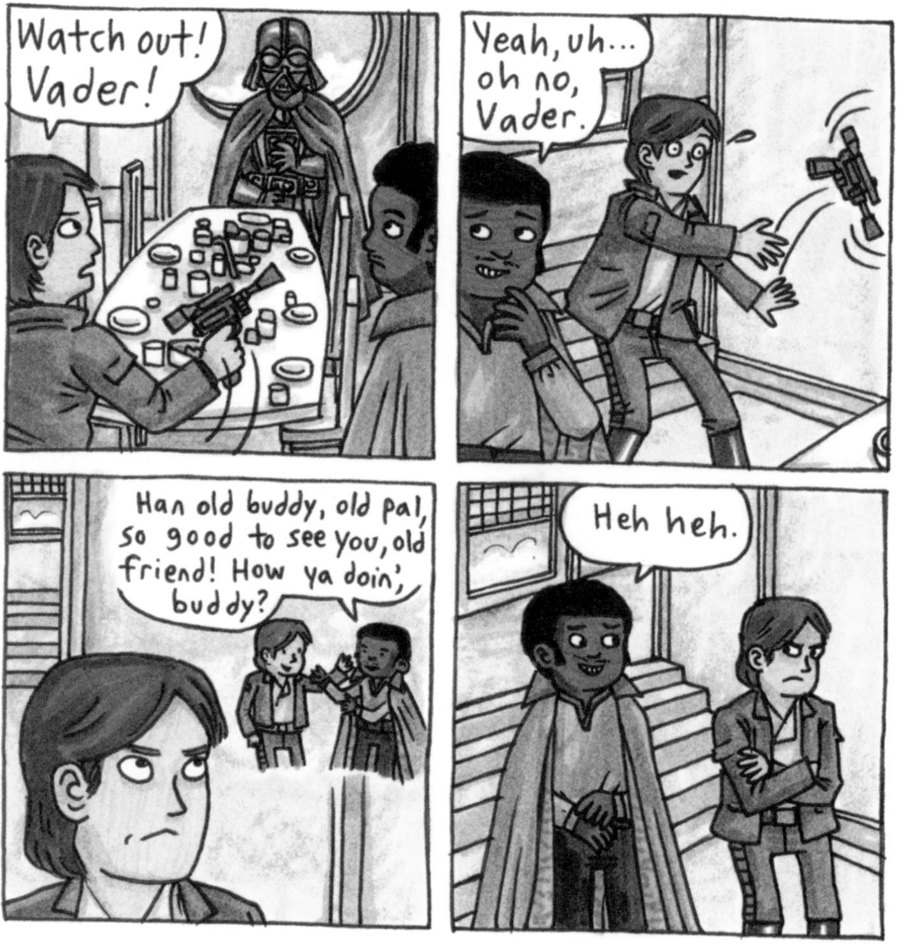
Watch out! Vader!
Yeah, uh... oh no, Vader.
Han old buddy, old pal, so good to see you, old friend! How ya doin', buddy?
Heh heh.

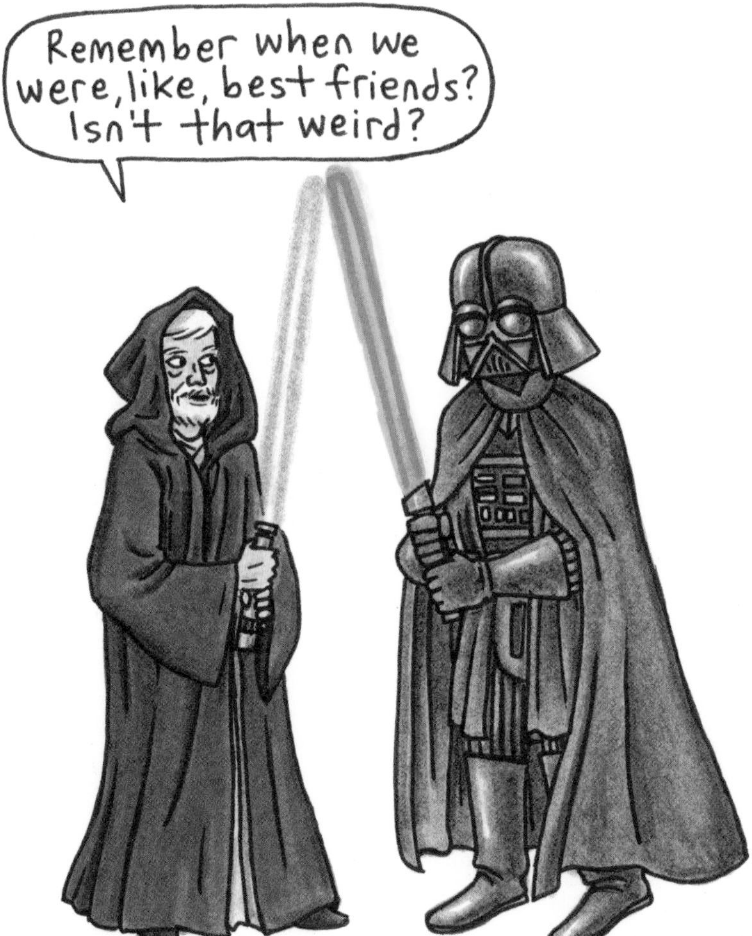
Remember when we were, like, best friends? Isn't that weird?

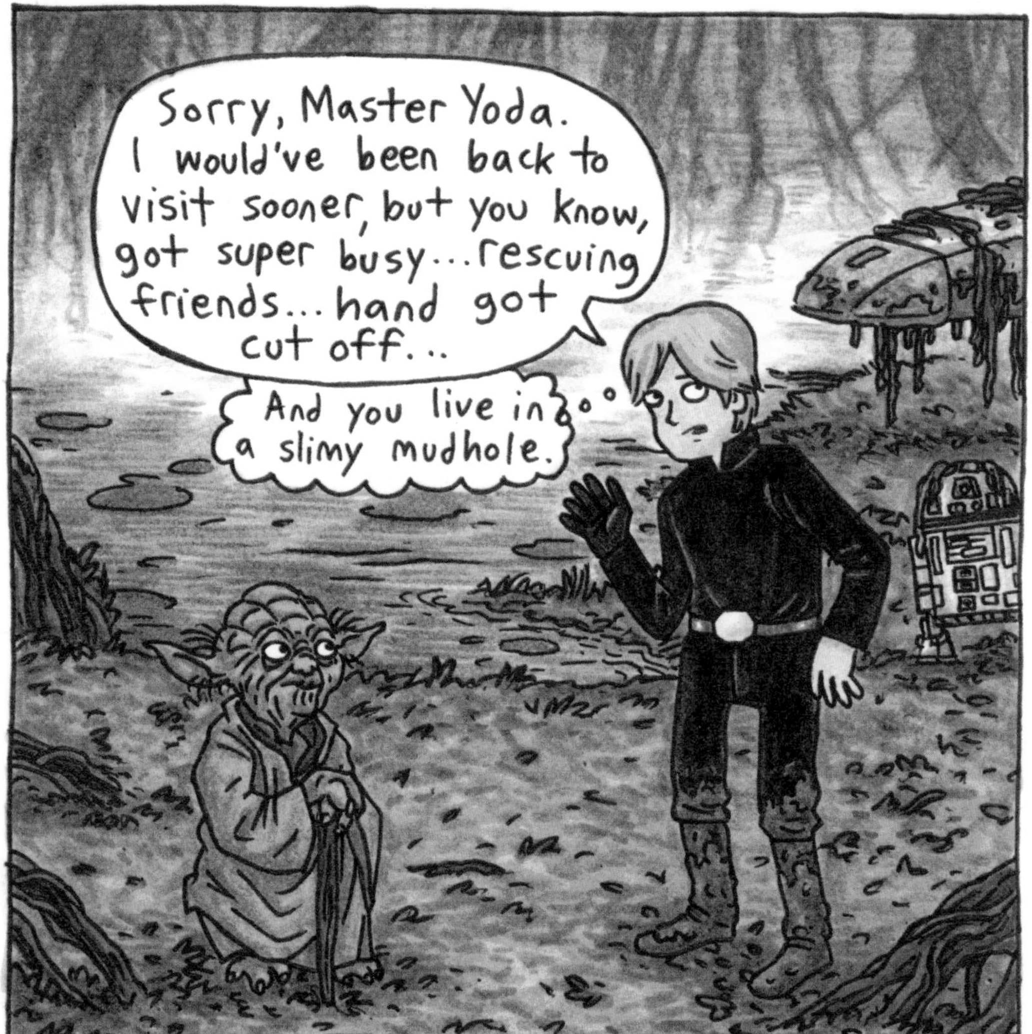

Sorry, Master Yoda. I would've been back to visit sooner, but you know, got super busy...rescuing friends...hand got cut off...
And you live in a slimy mudhole.

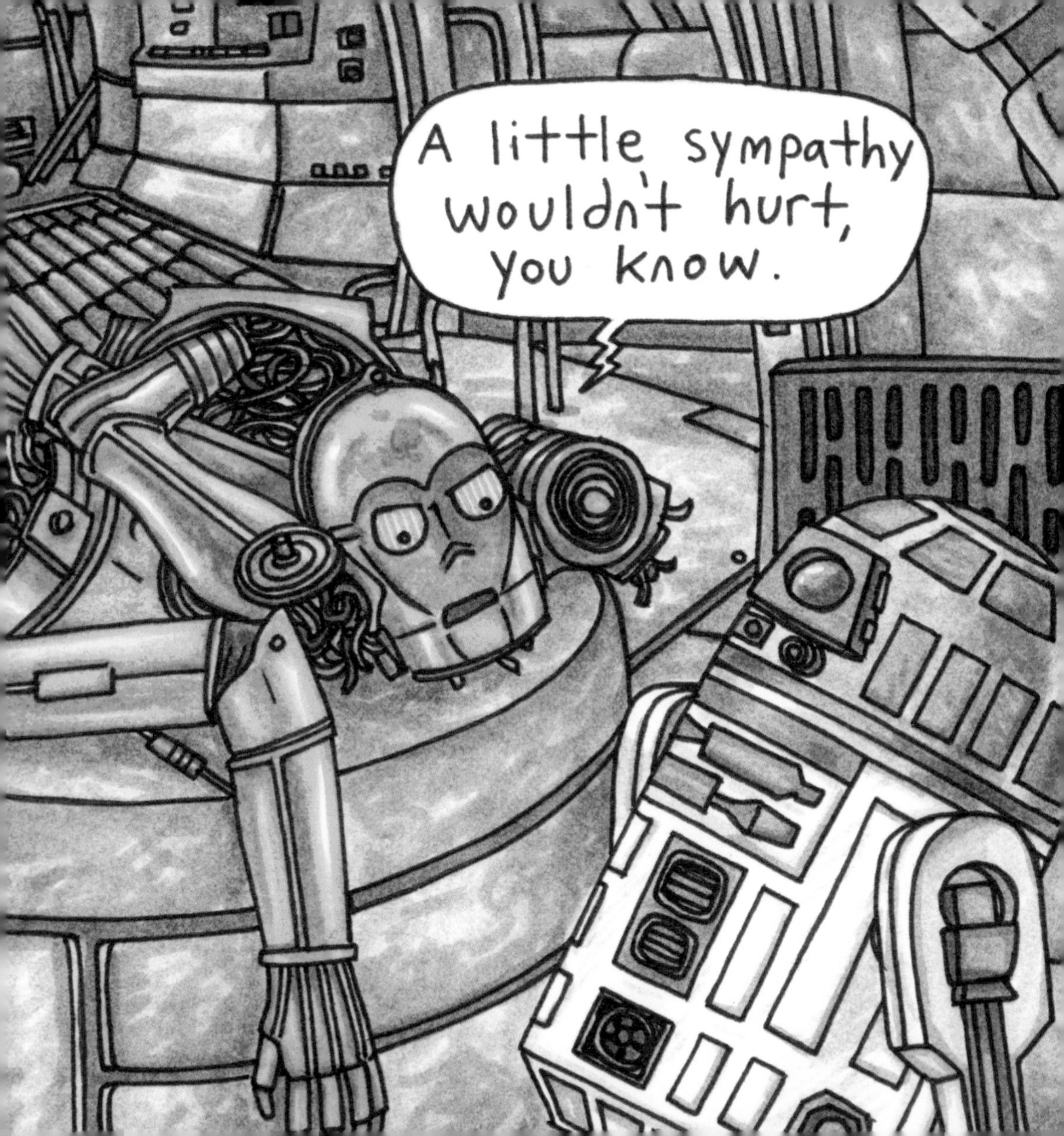
A little sympathy wouldn't hurt, you know.

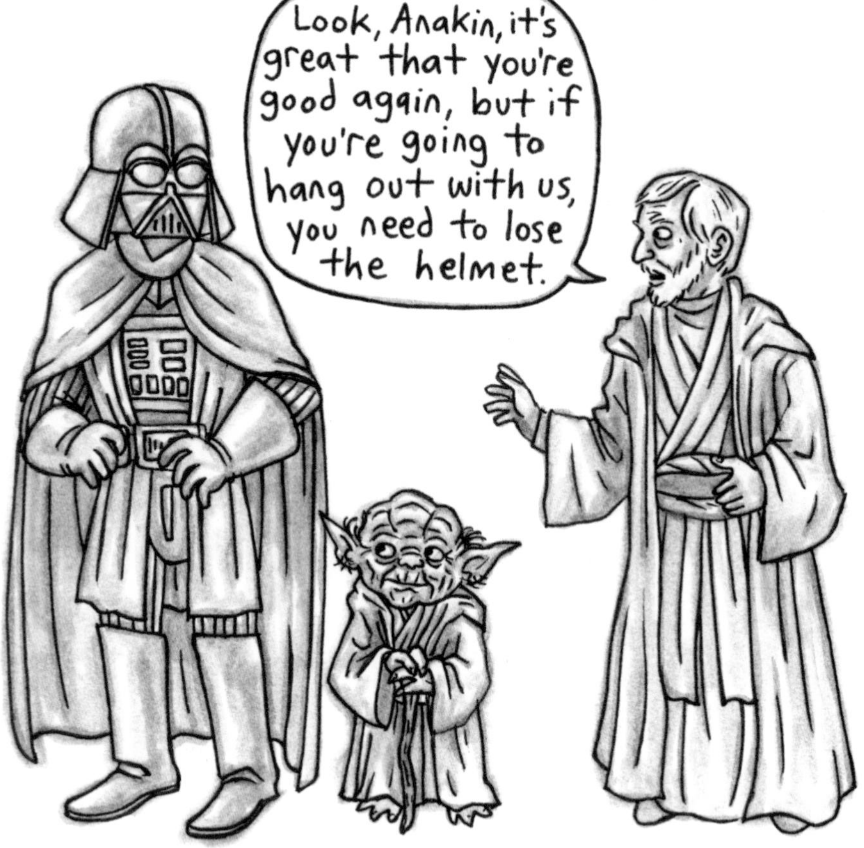
Look, Anakin, it's great that you're good again, but if you're going to hang out with us, you need to lose the helmet.

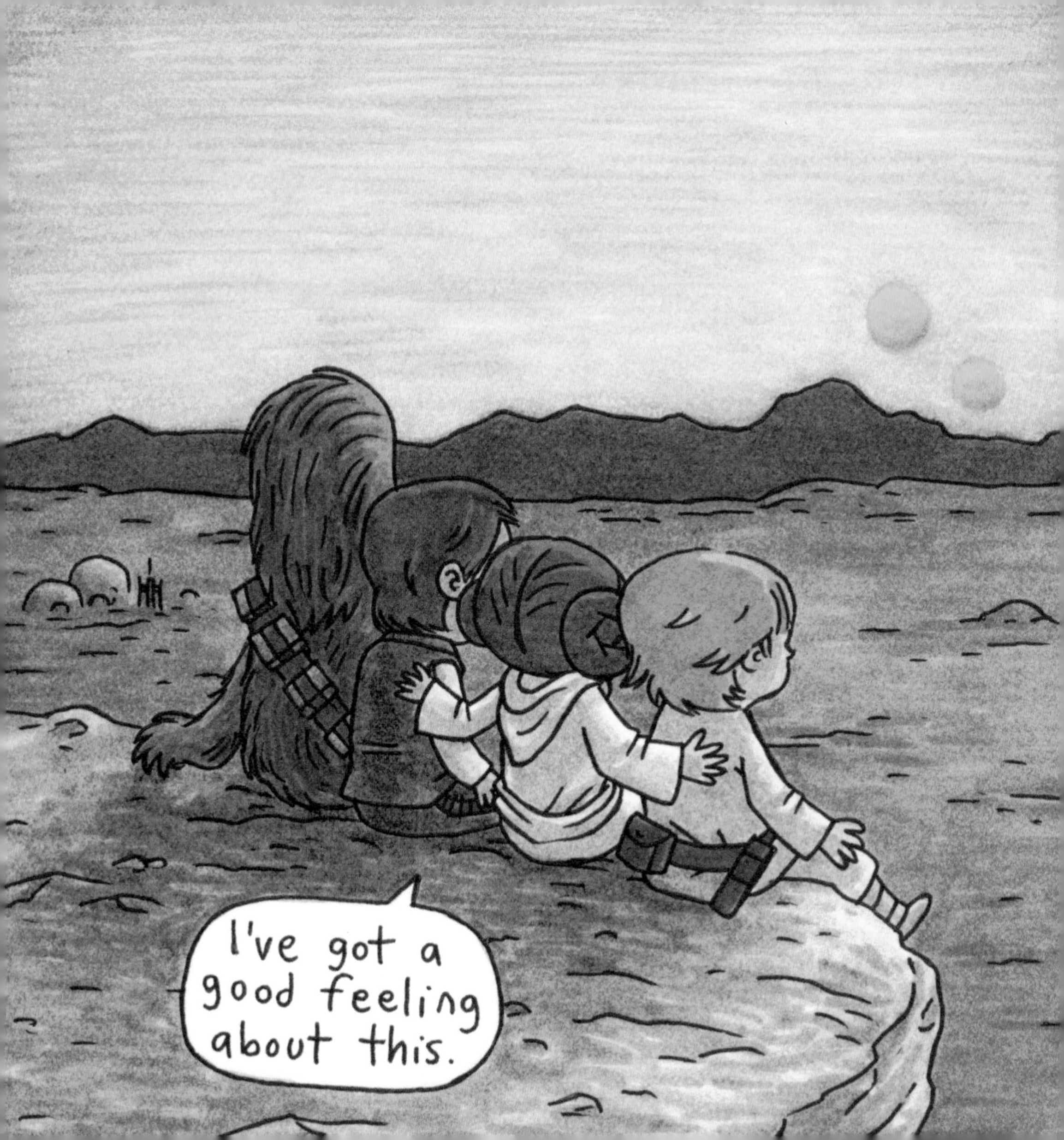
I've got a good feeling about this.

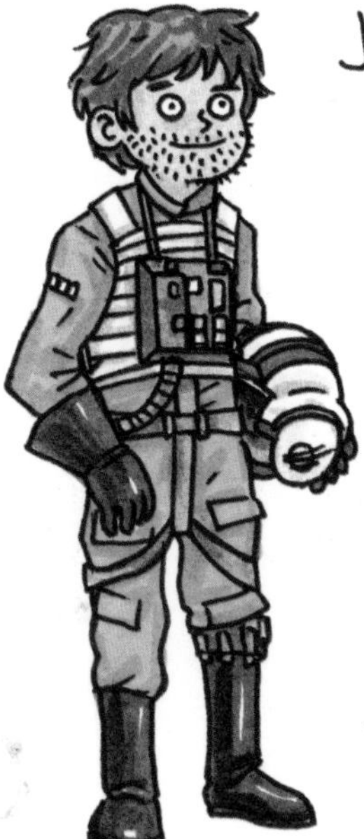

Jeffrey Brown is the author of numerous autobiographical comics, humorous graphic novels, and bestselling Star Wars books. He lives in Chicago with his wife and two sons.

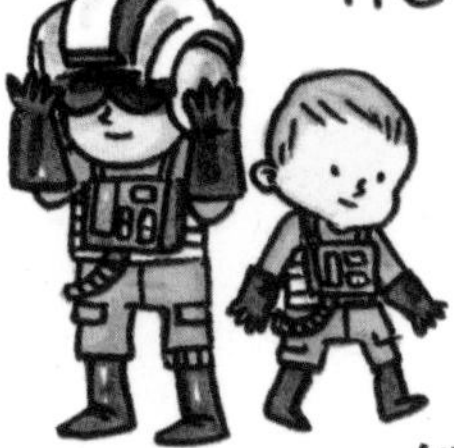

P.O. Box 120
Deerfield, IL 60015-0120
U.S.A.

WWW.JEFFREYBROWNCOMICS.COM

ALSO BY JEFFREY BROWN FROM CHRONICLE BOOKS:

Goodnight Darth Vader
Kids Are Weird
Vader's Little Princess
Darth Vader and Son
Cats Are Weird
Cat Getting Out of A Bag

www.chroniclebooks.com

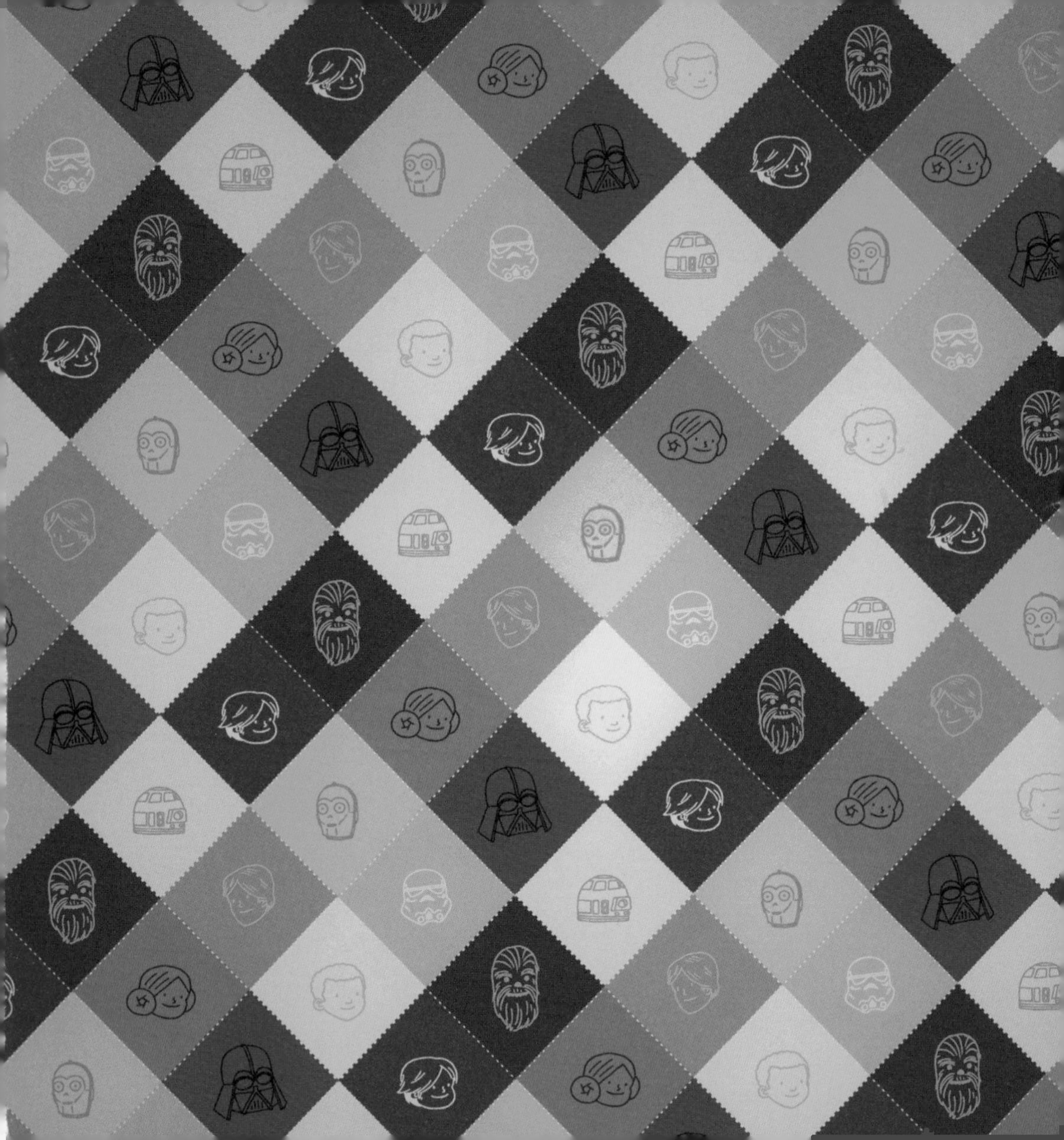

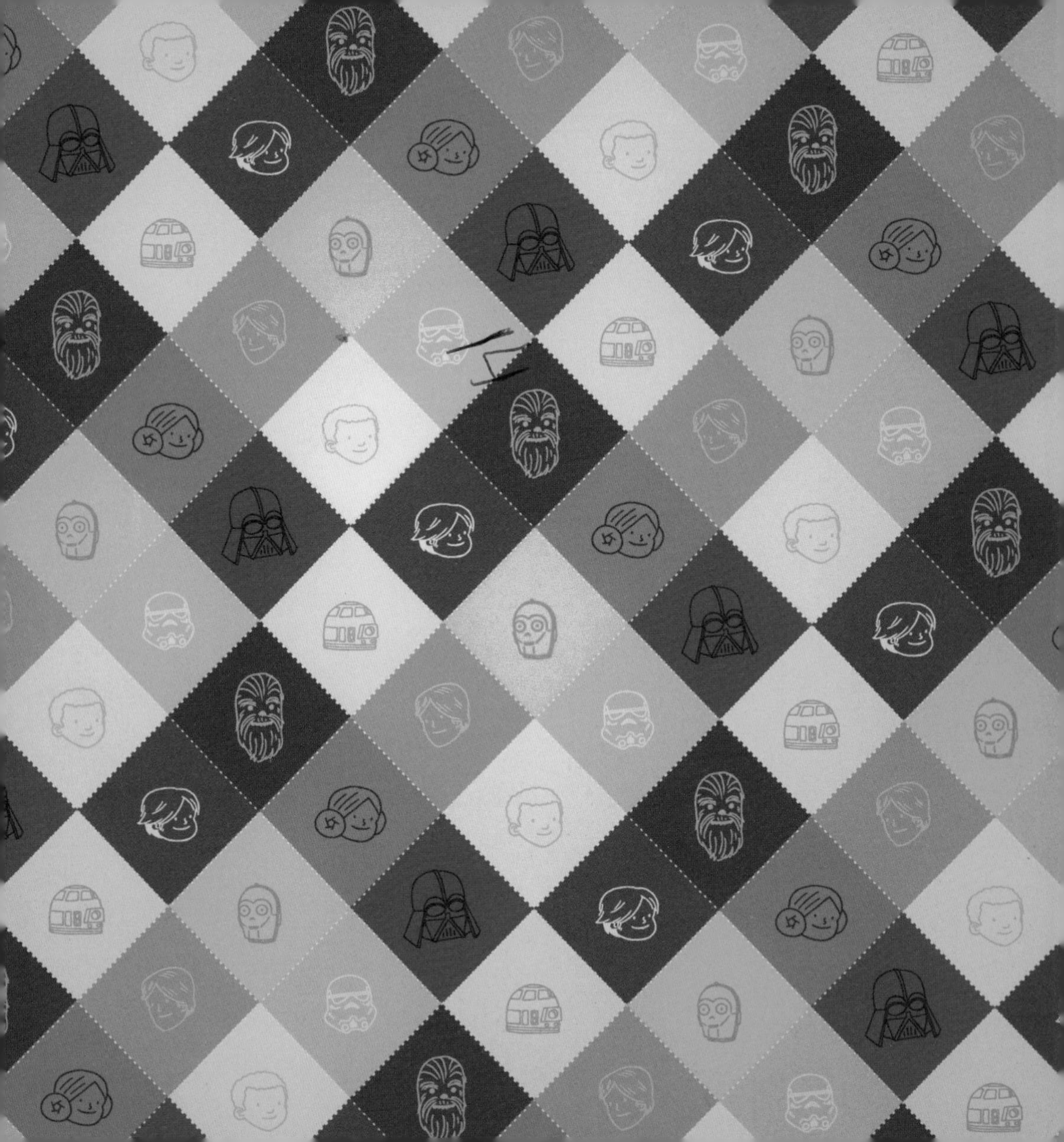